COLLINS

COLOURED KEY
to the
WILDFOWL
OF THE WORLD

By Peter Scott

in association with
THE WILDFOWL & WETLANDS TRUST

A *Key to the Wildfowl of the World* containing black-and-white drawings only, was first published in the 2nd Annual Report of the Severn Wildfowl Trust, 1948–49. It was reprinted as a separate book in 1950, revised and reprinted again in 1951.

This coloured version first published in 1957 amounts to an entirely new publication. Substantial additions have been made to the text and there has been further extensive revision in the light of the most recent taxonomic opinion.

Revised and reprinted 1961
Further revision, 1965, 1968, 1972
Reprinted 1977
Further revision 1988

This revised edition first published in 1998

03 02 01 00 99 98

14 13 12 11 10 9 8

ISBN 0 00 220110 0

Cover subject: Red-breasted Goose by Peter Scott

Colour origination by Colourscan Overseas Co. Pte. Ltd.
Printed and bound in Hong Kong by Printing Express Ltd.

FOREWORD

Wildfowl have a very particular charm. Their grace in the water, their perky deportment on land, the stunning variety of their colours during the breeding season, win them many devotees. No one during his lifetime did more to champion them than Sir Peter Scott. His paintings of them in wild and marshy landscapes captivated generation after generation of admirers – and still do. The ingenious techniques he devised to bring people and ducks – even wild ducks – close together, which he first developed at Slimbridge, led to the establishment of many similar reserves in Britain and countless others right around the world. And his scientific illustrations enabled anyone, anywhere, to identify any wildfowl he or she happened to encounter.

No single person was more responsible than Sir Peter for alerting the world to the urgent and vital need for nature conservation. Throughout his life he laboured tirelessly to protect animals and plants of all kinds. Even so, I suspect that had he been forced to pick one group of animals of which he was specially fond, it would have been the birds to which this book is such a vivid and lovely guide. It was first published some 50 years ago and it is good to see that after being updated scientifically it is being republished to aid and delight another generation. But that is not surprising – for I do not see how it could be bettered.

Sir David Attenborough, C.B.E., F.R.S.

A Coloured Key to the Wildfowl of the World
by Peter Scott

In the ten years since the last revision of the Key, a number of wildfowl have become extremely scarce and must be threatened with extinction, while one species, Madagascar White-eye (Plate 17), having not been certainly seen since 1991, and one sub-species, Niceforo's Pintail (Plate 9), not reported since 1952, are almost certainly now extinct.

There have been a few taxonomic changes since the last revision. A new sub-species of the White-fronted Goose, Elgas's Goose (Plate 3), has been described and the Mottled Duck (Plate 11) is now once more generally regarded as a separate race. The New Zealand Blue Duck (Plate 13)has been split into two races, but the formerly separated two races of the Bewick's Swan (Plate 2), Blue-winged Teal (Plate 12), Harlequin Duck (Plate 21) and Red-breasted Merganser (Plate 22) are now more frequently lumped together. It is still being debated whether the Cereopsis Geese (Plate 8) of Recherche Island belong to a separate race.

CONTENTS

ACKNOWLEDGEMENT

I would like to record my thanks to Hugh Boyd who originally helped to compile the introductory key and the index. I would also like to thank Malcolm Ogilvie for his recent updating of the text for this edition and Alison Byard for the information on the Wildfowl & Wetlands Trust which she has had to prepare in her own time, and my daughter Dafila Scott for lending her painting of the Red-breasted Goose on the cover.

Lady Philippa Scott

INTRODUCTION

In this Key there is a coloured picture of every kind of duck, goose or swan so far known to exist in the world – 245 kinds. The object of the book is to enable anyone, even without previous experience, to identify any bird within this group (called the family Anatidae) which they may see, and to discover its geographical range. It assumes that the bird has been seen at reasonably close quarters on the ground or on the water. The illustrations mainly show the birds in full breeding plumage. From June until October the drakes of many of the species of ducks from the Northern Hemisphere go into a dull 'eclipse plumage', which includes the period when the flight feathers are moulted and the birds are flightless. In this eclipse plumage the male in most cases looks very much like the female. The appearance of the females shows no striking change during the year, although it is sometimes affected by wear and tear of the feathers.

Where only one bird is shown as representative of each kind, as in the swans, geese, whistling ducks, etc., the sexes are virtually the same in plumage or, as in certain species of ducks, very similar but with the females slightly duller. In a few cases the female is so similar to that of a closely allied race that she is omitted in order to save space.

In the Key that follows and against the birds in the plates the conventional signs have been used to indicate sex, thus:

$\male$ = male $\female$ = female
$\male\male$ = males $\female\female$ = females

HOW TO USE THIS KEY

Each plate shows a group of species which are regarded as being particularly closely related so that in general the birds most likely to be confused with one another are shown on the same page. As a quick guide a certain number of basic characters such as size, shape, colour, behaviour and voice may give a clue to the page you want.

See, first of all, whether you can allocate the bird you are trying to identify to one or more of the headings on the following pages, and then see if you can trace it to a particular plate. Once you have the right plate there should be no great difficulty in making a final identification.

Relative sizes

VERY SMALL
Hottentot Teal

SMALL
Cape Teal

MEDIUM-SIZED
Mallard

RATHER LARGE
Shelduck

LARGE
Greylag Goose

VERY LARGE
Whistling Swan

1 Size

Very Large

Swans white, or white with black head and neck, or black, young grey or light brown 2

Large races of **Canada Goose** brown with black head and neck and white cheeks 5

Spur-winged Goose ♂♂ black and white, rather ugly 19

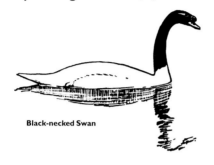

Black-necked Swan

Large

True Geese: 'Black Geese', 'Grey Geese', Snow Geese, Emperor and **Barhead** 3, 4, 5

Sheldgeese long legs, upright stance and **Steamer Ducks** heavy bills 6, 7, 8

Magpie Goose black and white, untidy-looking 1

White-winged Wood Duck, Muscovy Duck long body, short legs 19

Comb Duck ♂♂ black with white head and breast, head spotted with black, comb on bill 19

Spur-winged Goose ♀♀ black and white 19

Muscovy Duck

Rather Large

Eider

Very Small

Cotton Teal or
Indian Pygmy Goose

Small

Ruddy Duck

Medium

All the rest.

Pintail

2. Shape

Long Neck

Swans white, or white with black head and neck, or
black, young grey or light brown 2

Magpie Goose black and white, legs orange-yellow,
bill dirty yellowish, feet scarcely webbed 1

Spur-winged Goose black and white, legs flesh, bill
dark red. 19

Pink-headed Duck probably extinct 13

Long Legs

Whistling Ducks noisy, sociable, addicted to
perching on trees and posts 1

Hawaiian Goose brownish-grey with buff neck and
black head, feet only partially webbed. 5

Orinoco Goose fawn and brown, dark wings,
cherry-red legs, 'wind-swept' neck, very upright stance 6

Sheldgeese rather large, upright stance, small bills,
most forms finely barred black on sides and breast 7

Cape Barren Goose large, grey, with green bill,
pink legs and black feet, grunts like a pig 8

Spur-winged Goose very large, black and white,
dark red bill and legs. 19

Elongated Body

Black-necked Swan very large, white with black
head and neck, bright red knob on bill 2

Crested Ducks rather large, spotty brown, long
black tail, inconspicuous crest at back of head 8

African Black Ducks medium-sized, dark brown,
black backs with white spots 11

Hartlaub's, Muscovy and **White-winged
Wood Ducks** large or rather large, short legs. 19

Sawbills long, thin bills, mostly black and white or
brown and grey 22

Torrent Ducks pointed bills, upright stance,
long tails 14

PLATE Nº

Short Rounded Body

Eiders rather large, females brown, males black and white with brightly-coloured heads and necks 15

Goldeneyes and **Bufflehead** medium-sized and very small, males, black and white females dark brown heads, dive often 21

Stifftails mostly rather small, with broad bills, spiky tails carried flat on water or cocked well up, dive often 23

Long Tail

Crested Ducks rather large, mottled brown 8

Pintails and **Salvadori's Duck** medium-sized or rather small 9

Torrent Ducks medium-sized, tail broad as well as long, upright stance 14

Long-tailed Duck ♂ medium-sized, black and white 21

Stifftails mostly rather small, dive often 23

Crest at Back of Head

Tufted Duck

Tufted Duck ♂ black and white, dives freely 17

Falcated Duck

Falcated Duck ♂ iridescent bronze head 10

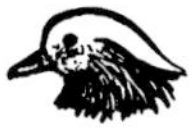

Mandarin

Carolina or Wood Duck

Mandarin and **Carolina Ducks** males with larger crests, and very brightly coloured 18

Crested Shelduck

Crested Shelduck rather large, long legs, probably extinct 6

Crested Duck

Crested Ducks rather large, long tail, mottled brown 8

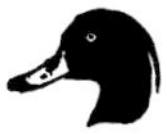

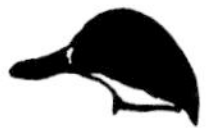

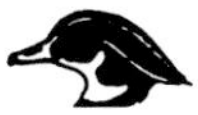

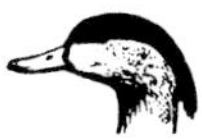

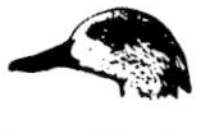

Marbled Teal small, beige-coloured with soft black spots, crest inconspicuous 9

Marbled Teal

Mergansers long thin bills. 22

Red-breasted Merganser

Hooded Merganser

Goosander ♀♀ long thin bills, chestnut heads 22

Smew ♂ nearly white 22

Smew

Tuft on crown

Red-crested Pochard ♂ crown orange, like shaving-brush 16

Red-crested Pochard

Cuban and **Spotted Whistling Ducks** long legs, flanks spotted with white, tuft inconspicuous 1

3. Bill Shape

Long thin bill, hooked at tip

Goosander, **Merganser** and **Smew** (Sawbills) 22

Goosander ♀

Torrent Ducks bills bright red 14

Torrent Duck

Long, broad, spoon-shaped

Shovelers medium-sized 12

Shoveler

Long with flaps at tip

Pink-eared Duck small, light brownish-grey with fine black bars. 13

Pink-eared Duck

Making straight line with forehead

Swan Goose

Swans very large 2

Swan Goose large, with black bill and dark brown
stripe down back of neck 3

Eider

Eiders rather large, males black and white with
coloured heads, females brown 15

Canvasback medium-sized – larger than **Pochard** or
Redhead, dives often 16

Comb or knob above bill

Mute Swan very large, white, orange-pink bill,
knob black. 2

Black-necked Swan white with black head and neck,
knob red 2

Domestic Chinese Goose large, upright stance,
imperious look, belly nearly touches ground 3

Comb Duck

Comb Duck or **Knob-nosed Goose** ♂
rather large, white head with black spots, knob black. 19

Muscovy Duck ♂ large, black glossed with green.
Domestic forms white, grey or black, or mixtures,
knob black or red. 19

Rosybill ♂ medium-sized, black and grey with
cherry-red bill. 16

Some **Scoter** ♂♂ medium-sized, glossy black 20

White-headed Stifftail ♂ bill blue, dives often 23

King Eider

King Eider ♂ medium-sized, black with pink breast,
blue-grey head, knob orange. 15

Lobe hanging under bill

Musk Duck

Musk Duck ♂ rather large, sooty dark grey,
dives often 23

Down-curved bill

Blue Duck

Blue Duck medium-sized, grey, with
flesh-coloured bill 13

Cape Barren Goose

Cape Barren Goose large, grey, with greenish bill 8

Very large, heavy bill

Steamer Duck

Steamer Ducks large, grey marked with brown 8

Thick-billed Bean Goose

Thick-billed Bean Goose large, brownish-grey, orange band on bill and orange legs 3

Eastern Greylag Goose large, pale brownish-grey, bill and legs pink 3

4. Colour

Very bright with complex pattern

Red-breasted Goose medium-sized, black, sharply marked with chestnut and white 5

Baikal Teal ♂ small, with black, green, buff and white on head 10

Mandarin Duck ♂ medium-sized, with orange hackles and 'sails', white stripe on head 18

Carolina or **Wood Duck** ♂ medium-sized, with glossy green and white head, purple breast, scarlet eye, orange bill 18

African Pygmy Goose ♂ small, chestnut breast and flanks, green patch on side of head, bright orange bill 18

King Eider ♂ medium-sized, black and white, with pink breast, blue-grey and pale green patches on head, orange-red bill 15

Steller's Eider ♂ small, black and white, chestnut below shading to orange-pink, green patches on head 15

Harlequin Duck ♂ medium-sized, blue-grey and white with chestnut flanks and sandy-orange stripe over eye 21

White

Swans very large, long-necked 2

Snow Geese large, pink bill and legs, black wing-tips 4

Kelp Goose ♂ large, black bill and yellow legs, all plumage pure white 7

Nearly white

Magellan or **Upland Geese** ♂♂ large, upright
stance, barred flanks, grey backs 7

Smew small, white, with some black markings on
head and back, thin, rather pointed bill 22

Immatures of **Swans**, **Snow Geese** and **Kelp Geese** 2, 4, 7

Black

Black Swan very large, long-necked, with white
wing-tips. 2

Muscovy Duck large, short-legged, black with green
or purple gloss, white patch on wing 19

Scoter ♂♂ medium-sized ducks, black with
coloured bill. 20

New Zealand Shelduck ♂ rather large, long-legged, with
green and white in wing 6

Sharply black-and-white

Black-necked Swan very large, white, with
black neck. 2

Magpie Goose large, white with black head,
neck and wings. 1

Common Shelduck rather large, white with black
head, neck and wings, chestnut band on breast, red bill 6

Goosander ♂♂ rather large, white with black head
and back, long hook-tipped bill. 22

Eider ♂♂ rather large, with white shoulders, white
or pink breast, black body, green patches on head 15

Tufted and **Ring-necked Duck** ♂♂ medium-sized
diving ducks with black heads, necks and bodies, white
or pale grey sides 17

Common and **Barrow's Goldeneye** ♂♂
medium-sized diving ducks with black heads,
white breasts, flanks and some white on the back,
white spot in front of eye 21

Chestnut

Ruddy Shelduck rather large, nearly uniformly
coloured, with paler head, black tail and wing-tips 6

Pink Head

Orange Head

5 Brightly-coloured Bills

Red Bill

Mandarin Duck ♂ medium-sized duck with orange hackles and 'sails', white stripe on head 18

Red Spot on Bill

Bahama Pintail warm brown with dark crown and white cheeks, bill blue with red spot at base 9

Indian and **Burma Spotbills** pale mallards with white in wing, yellow tip to bill and red spot at base 11

Orange Bill

Pacific, **Northern** or **King Eider** ♂♂ rather large black and white duck. 15

White-winged Wood Duck rather large, blackish-brown with spotty white head and spotty bill. 19

African Pygmy Goose small duck, dark green above and chestnut on breast and flanks. 18

Western Greylag Goose large brownish-grey bird with pinkish legs. 3

Bean Geese large brownish-grey birds with orange legs and some black on bill. 3

Carolina or **Wood Duck** ♂ medium-sized duck with glossy green and white head, purple breast, scarlet eye 18

Yellow Bill

Magpie Goose large black and white, bill variously covered with dark scaly spots 1

Bar-headed Goose large pale grey goose with black bars over head. 4

Spectacled Eider ♂ rather large black and white duck with pale green on head 15

Greenland Whitefront rather large dark brown goose with white forehead and orange legs 3

Abyssinian and **African Yellowbills** medium-sized dark brown mottled ducks with black stripe down centre of bright yellow bill 11

Green Bill

Cape Barren Goose large grey goose with green top to bill 8

European, **American** or **Faeroe Eider** rather
large ducks, with long, high bills 15

Mallard ♂♂ glossy green heads, maroon breasts,
or plain brown with spots in some races 11

Blue Bill

Stifftail or **Ruddy Duck** ♂♂ small diving ducks,
round in shape with chestnut bodies, black heads with
or without white cheeks 23

Puna Teal medium-sized grey duck with black crown
and white cheeks, black line along centre of bill 9

Silver Teal small grey teal with black crown, cream
cheeks, black line along centre of bill and yellow spot
at base in ♂ , sometimes in ♀ 9

Hottentot Teal very small brownish duck with black
crown, cream cheeks with a dark patch 9

Ringed Teal ♂ very small duck with creamy grey
cheeks, pink breast, chestnut on sides of back 13

Philippine Duck medium-sized grey duck with light
chestnut face and sharp eye-stripe. 11

Bahama and **Galapagos Pintails** medium or small,
brown, white cheeks, red spot at base of bill 9

Black-necked Swan very large white bird with black
head and neck and red knob above blue bill 2

Red-breasted Goose

6.Voice

Trumpeting or bugling

Trumpeter, **Whooper**, **Whistling** and
Bewick's Swans very large white birds 2

Honking

True Geese very large or large birds, brown- or grey-,
or black-and-white, or white 3, 4, 5

Whistling

Barking

Quacking

Dabbling Duck ♀♀ medium-sized or small,
mainly brown 9, 10, 11, 12

Clucking

Baikal Teal ♂ small, with bronze-green and buff
patterning on head 10

Shoveler ♂ small, with very large bill 12

Rattling or nattering

Radjah Shelduck ♀ medium-sized, white, with pale
pink bill and legs, reddish brown or dark brown on back 6

Crested Duck ♀ rather large mottled brown with
long tail and a small crest 8

Bronze-winged Duck ♀ medium-sized, brown
with white crescent on face and white patch under chin 9

Garganey ♂ small, white stripe above eye, brown
head, pale grey flanks, greyish back, sounds like
fishing reel 12

Blue-winged Teal ♂ small, mottled red-brown,
grey head with white crescent on side of face 12

Cinnamon Teal ♂ small, deep chestnut, with sky-
blue shoulders (usually hidden) 12

Smew ♂ small white bird with black markings
on head and back, thin sharp bill 22

Grunting

Cape Barren Goose ♀ large, grey, with green bill,
pink legs and black feet 8

Gadwall ♂ medium-sized grey and brown duck with
black under tail 12

Laughing

Common Shelduck ♀ rather large, black and
white, red bill, red-brown band across breast 6

Hissing

Mute Swan very large, white, orange and black bill 2

Egyptian Goose ♂ large grey bird with chestnut
brown markings, including patch round yellow eye 6

Muscovy Duck ♂ large black duck with black or
red lumpy bill, sounds like small steam engine 19

True Geese in defence 3, 4, 5

7. Behaviour

Frequent Diving

Male Goldeneye

Torrent Ducks medium-sized, slim build, with long stiff tails, red bills and feet 14

Pochards medium-sized, ♂♂ smartly marked, females brown 16, 17

Eiders rather large, or medium-sized, ♂♂ black and white with coloured heads, ♀♀ brown, both sexes with large bills 15

Scoters medium-sized, ♂♂ black, ♀♀ brown 20

Harlequins, Longtail and **Goldeneyes** medium-sized or smaller, mostly black- or brown-and-white 21

Sawbills black-and-white or grey-and-white, with long thin, pointed or hooked bills 22

Stifftails small or very small, 'tubby', ♂♂ chestnut, black and white, with blue bills, ♀♀ brown 23

Whistling Ducks (sometimes) medium-sized or small, with long legs and necks 1

Grazing

Red-breasted Goose

Swans very large white or black and white birds 2

True Geese very large or large, brown-, or grey-, or black-and-white, or white 3, 4, 5

Sheldgeese large, long-legged, with small bills, white or brown, with black barring on flanks, and sometimes on breast 7

Wigeon medium-sized ducks, ♂♂ brightly-coloured with white or buff crowns. ♀♀ duller 12

Australian Wood Duck ♂ grey with chocolate head, ♀ mottled grey and brown 18

Perching on branches, posts, etc.

Red-billed Whistling Duck

Magpie Goose large, black and white, orange yellow legs and bill 1

Whistling Ducks medium-sized or small, long legs, upright stance 1

Radjah Shelduck medium-sized, white with pink bill and feet, dark brown back and breast band 6

Orinoco Goose very upright, neck 'wind-swept', fawn, with chestnut flanks, greenish-black wings, cherry-red legs 6

Green-winged Teal small, ♂♂ with brown and green head and grey-brown body, ♀♀ brown 9

White-winged Wood and **Muscovy Ducks** large, rather ugly, black with white patches 19

Spur-winged Goose very large, very ugly, black and white, with dark red bill and legs 19

Mutual Preening

White-faced Whistling Duck rather small, long-legged, upright stance 1

Orinoco Goose rather large, upright stance, fawn with chestnut flanks, greenish-black wings and cherry-red legs 6

Mandarin and **Carolina Ducks** small, ♂♂ improbably and brilliantly coloured with crests, ♀♀ greyish-brown, mottled underneath 18

White-faced Whistling Ducks

IF YOU ARE STUCK

If you are unable to identify your bird from the Key or from the Plates the following possibilities should then be carefully considered.

The bird may be:

1 An immature specimen, the plumage of which is likely to be similar to the female, or intermediate between that of the male and female.

2 A male in eclipse plumage of one of the species in which the drake spends several months in a dull plumage usually resembling the female. Intermediate plumages occur during the transition.

3 A hybrid. These are comparatively frequent in wildfowl and the parentage is not always apparent even to an expert eye.

4 A variety or freak, showing white in patches (schizochromism) or a uniform paleness of plumage (leucism) or blackness (melanism). Pure albinism – pure white with pink eyes – has very rarely been recorded in wildfowl.

5 Descended from domestic stock. Such birds, capable of flight, include some tame grey or white or 'skewbald' geese (from Greylag stock) and Chinese Geese (Plate 3). Much more frequently mistaken for wild birds, however, are various forms of the Mallard (Plate 11) which show domestic blood and the domestic form of the Muscovy Duck (Plate 18), all of which may be quite good fliers.

Mallards showing domestic blood may take the following forms:

(i) White Call Ducks (small; white with yellow or orange bill)

(ii) Cayuga Ducks (medium-sized; black or dark reddish-brown, with black head and variable-sized white patch on breast.)[1]

---

1 It has not yet been established whether these birds, which are not uncommon, are descended from domestic 'Cayuga' type stock or whether they represent a fairly frequent mutation capable of arising from perfectly wild stock.

(iii) Mallards with white wing-tips, broad white neck-rings, etc.

Muscovy Ducks with domestic blood can be:

(iv) Black glossed with green; white in wings; variable additional white, most often on head; bill swollen and bright red or black and red.

(v) Pure white with red bill.

(vi) Pale grey, usually with white head and red bill.

(vii) Mixtures of all three colours.

If you have seen a striking duck or goose which you cannot trace from this Key or from the Plates, it is very likely to be a Muscovy Duck, or a Mallard showing domestic blood, or a hybrid – in that order of probability.

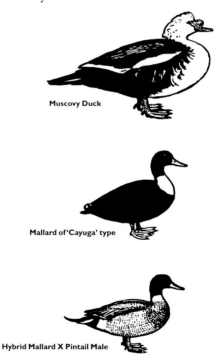

Muscovy Duck

Mallard of 'Cayuga' type

Hybrid Mallard X Pintail Male

NAMES AND CLASSIFICATION

All the birds in this book are given at least two names. Those printed in bold type are the English, or vernacular, names. The choice of these names is not governed by strict rules of procedure and people differ more or less strongly in their preferences. The ones used here are for the most part those in general use in ornithological hand-books. For species found in Britain these are the same as the 'common' names, used by wildfowlers and birdwatchers and those with just a general interest in the birds around them. But the text-book names given to species occurring elsewhere, in Australia for example, do not necessarily coincide with the names used locally. This Key tries to include the most widely-used of such local names, though confining itself to English ones.

The names printed in italic type are those applied to the different kinds of birds according to the formal procedure of taxonomy. It may be helpful to explain briefly the significance and use of such names. Taxonomy, the study of the principles of classification of animals (and plants), has two distinct components, classification and nomenclature. *Classification* deals with the ranking of various categories (such as family, genus, species) to which organisms are assigned in accordance with their evolutionary relationships, and *nomenclature* deals with the legalistic aspect of names (which name should properly be used for a given animal, according to the International Code of Zoological Nomenclature).

Classification has a double purpose. From a practical point of view, a system of grouping makes it easier to identify animals. From a theoretical point of view a 'natural' classification shows, to some extent, the relationships or supposed relationships of the groups concerned and helps to indicate the course which evolution has taken.

The system of classification applied to animals may best be demonstrated by means of examples taken from the text opposite Plate 1. The groups used are in a hierarchy, in which any category includes all the subsequent (lower) categories. The six universally recognised categories, in descending order of rank, are: Phylum, Class, Order, Family, Genus and Species. This system is expanded according to the needs of specialists in any group by using the prefixes 'super-' and 'sub-'. Birds belong to the Phylum *Chordata* (which includes all vertebrate animals and those animals without vertebrae which possess a notochord) and form the Class *Aves*. The swans, geese and ducks are included in the Order *Anseriformes*, one of twenty-three orders into which the Class *Aves* is divided. The Order *Anseriformes* includes the Family *Anhimidae* (the Screamers) and the family *Anatidae* (Swans, geese and ducks.)[1]

The Family *Anatidae* is divided into three Sub-Families. The Magpie Goose (Plate 1) is considered so different from all other wildfowl in the details of its anatomy that it is assigned to the Sub-Family *Anseranatinae* while the remainder are assigned to the Sub-Families *Anserinae* (Swans, Geese and Whistling Ducks) or *Anatinae* (the remaining ducks). Delacour and Mayr, whose paper *The Family Anatidae* (Wilson Bulletin Vol. 57, No. 1, pp. 3–55, 1945) provides the basis of the classification adopted in this Key, insert a further category, the Tribe, between the Sub-Family and the Genus. They use the term tribe (with the ending *-ini*) for a recognisable group of genera within each sub-family. The Magpie Goose forms a Tribe, a genus and a species by itself.

The Sub-Family *Anserinae* is divided by Delacour and Mayr into two tribes, *Anserini* – the Swans and Geese, and *Dendrocygnini* – the Whistling Ducks (Plate 1). All the members of the Tribe *Dendrocygnini* are assigned to a single Genus, *Dendrocygna*. But the Tribe *Anserini* includes four genera, *Coscoroba*, *Cygnus*, *Anser* and *Branta*, while the Sub-Family *Anatinae* is divided into seven tribes and includes 34 genera.

This lack of numerical equivalence between the groups shows the complexity of the relationships within the Family. But though it is difficult to give any precise meaning to the concepts, there is a general belief that genera and above all species form comparable natural units, whether in birds or mammals, or invertebrates or

1 Some consider that the Family Phoenicopteridae (the Flamingoes) should also be included in the order Anseriformes.

plants. The scientific name of Magpie Goose is made up of the generic name *Anseranas* (Goose-duck) and the species name *semi-palmata* (half-webbed). This use of the combination of generic and specific names to describe the most important recognisable natural group – the species – is the principle of binomial nomenclature, first consistently applied by the great Swedish taxonomist Linnaeus in the middle of the eighteenth century.

All these long Latin names are subject to a strict set of rules of nomenclature. Only the method of choosing the generic and specific names will be illustrated here, although rules are also laid down for applying the correct names to higher groups. The first principle of naming a species is that a type specimen of the organism shall be described under that name. The description must be detailed enough to make clear what differences are supposed to exist between the named specimens and other rather similar animals, and the species must be provided with a type locality, wherever possible the place at which the type specimen was collected. It has frequently happened that someone has described an animal as of a new species only for it to be shown later that a similar animal had been described earlier by someone else, so that two (or more) names are available for the same species. To get over this difficulty there is a rule of priority. The first specific name applied to a species must stand, except in very special circumstances, which have to be argued for any particular case.

The generic name consists of a single word, printed with an initial capital. The specific name is also a single word, written with a small initial letter. These, and all scientific names, must be words which are either Latin or latinized or are treated as such in case they are not of classic origin. The original describer can choose what specific name he likes, providing it agrees grammatically with the generic name. Usually the names chosen refer to a feature of the bird's appearance, or where it lives, though sometimes the describer names an animal in honour of a friend, or another specialist in the same group, or the collector who obtained the type specimen.

Three words in a scientific name indicate that the species seems to be made up of several more or less distinct groups, separated geographically, which though sufficiently alike to justify them being regarded as a single species, show sufficient variation from group to group to enable most individuals to be identifiable as members of one subspecies rather than another. (Subspecies are sometimes referred to as 'races' and as 'forms', and in this context the three terms are almost synonymous, though 'form' would also include species which are not subdivided into subspecies or races.) One of the subspecies repeats the specific name, while the remainder are given additional names. Some examples may make this clearer.

The Whistling Ducks of Plate 1 illustrate all these points. The Spotted Whistling Duck is called *Dendrocygna guttata. Dendrocygna* means 'tree-duck' – a reference to the long-necked appearance of all members of the genus, and to their habit of perching on trees – and *guttata* means spotted. *Dendrocygna eytonis* is named for the man who discovered and described the species. (It is not now usual for a taxonomist to name a species after himself.) Both these species show no signs of geographical variation. But the Wandering Whistling Duck *Dendrocygna arcuata* (the specific name *arcuata*, arched or bowed, refers to the flank feathers) forms three geographical races or subspecies. The Wandering Whistling Ducks of the East Indies form one subspecies. Since the type specimen of the species came from this area this subspecies must be called *Dendrocygna arcuata arcuata*. Australian specimens are larger and can be recognised as *Dendrocygna arcuata australis*, while specimens from New Britain, which are a good deal smaller, are distinguishable as *D.a. pygmaea*. (When generic and specific names need to be referred to repeatedly they can be contracted to their initial letters for brevity.) You will notice in the text that it is uncertain to which race birds from New Caledonia should be allotted. This kind of overlap is frequently found. Sometimes fuller investigation enables a clear-cut decision to be made, but often it must be accepted that such birds are truly intermediate, in which case, though the forms at each end of the varying population are given distinct names, the intermediate birds cannot be given a trinominal name and may be treated as *D.a. australis* ↔ *pygmaea* or in some other inevitably clumsy way.

It will be noted that another name in Roman type follows the specific or subspecific name, e.g., *Dendrocygna guttata* Schlagel. This is the author's name. The author of a scientific name is the person who first publishes the name in connection with a description. The author's name is not always given as part of the scientific name, but is useful in making clear which type description is being used in cases where the history of the name is complicated. (There are uncomfortably many complications, because most names originate from 150 to 200 years ago, a period when first publications were often in obscure journals not widely circulated, so that species were often described as 'new' several times by different authors in the course of a few years.) Changing ideas about relationships have also caused the accepted limits of many species to vary. Changing ideas about relationships are responsible too for the presence or absence of parentheses enclosing the author's name. The rule is that the author's name appears without brackets if he originally described the species as a member of the genus in which it is now placed. But if the author placed it in another genus, then his name appears in brackets. For example, Eyton first described the Plumed Whistling Duck (in 1838) under the name *Leptotarsis eytoni*. Since it is now considered to belong to the genus *Dendrocygna*, *Leptotarsis eytoni* Eyton has been replaced by *Dendrocygna eytoni* (Eyton).

The contractions L. or (L.) which appear frequently instead of an author's name stand for Linneaus, the inaugurator of binomial nomenclature.

The 245 forms of swans, geese and ducks – all that are so far known to science – are comprised of 151 full species. Of these, 48 species, together with a further six subspecies, have been found in the wild in Britain. These are marked in the text thus *. Two of these, Greylag Goose and Canada Goose, also have substantial free-living breeding populations stemming from released or escaped birds, as do the non-native Egyptian Goose, Mandarin Duck and North American Ruddy Duck. Several other wildfowl, both on the British

List and species which have never reached here in the wild state, have much smaller breeding populations that have arisen in the same manner. Five species and four races believed to have become altogether extinct throughout the world in recent years are marked thus †.

SCALE OF THE PLATES

It should be noticed that five different scales have been used in the drawings – one for the swans (Plate 2), one for the True Geese and Sheldgeese (Plates 3, 4, 5, 7), one for the Shelducks and Perching Geese (Plates 6, 18), one for the Whistling Ducks, Crested and Steamer Ducks and Cape Barren Goose, and Scoters (Plates 1, 8, 20) and one for the rest of the ducks (Plates 9–17, 19, 21–23). This complication has arisen because, within the framework of the natural groupings, the birds have been drawn as large as possible in order to show the detail; teal would be too small to show the markings if drawn on the same scale as swans, all of which must be shown on one page.

Salvadori's Duck

TAXONOMIC CLASSIFICATION

Kingdom	**Animalia**
Phylum	**Chordata**
Class	**Aves**
Order	**Anseriformes**
Sub-order	**Anseres**
Family	**Anatidae**

PLATE I MAGPIE GOOSE AND WHISTLING OR TREE DUCKS

Sub-family **Anseranatinae**
Tribe **Anseranatini**

I Magpie Goose Anseranas semipalmata (LATHAM) Southern New Guinea and northern and south-eastern Australia.

Sub-family **Anserinae**
Tribe **Dendrocygnini**
(Whistling Ducks or Tree Ducks)

2 Spotted Whistling Duck Dendrocygna guttata SCHLEGEL Philippines (Mindanao), Indonesia (Sulawesi to New Guinea) and Papua New Guinea (including Bismarck Archipelago).

3 Plumed or **Eyton's Whistling Duck** Dendrocygna eytoni (EYTON) Australia, including Tasmania, but abundant only in the tropics.

4 East Indian Wandering Whistling Duck Dendrocygna arcuata arcuata (HORSFIELD) Philippines and Indonesia (Borneo to the Moluccas).

5 Australian Wandering Whistling Duck Dendrocygna arcuata australis REICHENBACK Tropical Australia and southern New Guinea. Birds in northern New Guinea (and formerly in New Caledonia) probably belong to this form, or are intermediate between it and pygmœa.

6 Lesser Wandering Whistling Duck Dendrocygna arcuata pygmaea MAYR New Britain where only very small numbers (and formerly Fiji Islands, where it has probably been exterminated by the introduction of the mongoose).

7 Fulvous Whistling Duck Dendrocygna bicolor (VIEILLOT) South from southern California and Texas to central Mexico; northern tropical South America from Colombia to Guyana and French Giana; Brazil, Peru, south to Paraguay and northern Argentina; East Africa from Lake Chad to Natal; Madagascar; India, Sri Lanka and Myanmar (Burma), south to Pegu. (This is a most extraordinary distribution for any species of bird. There is no geographical variation throughout this huge and broken range.)

8 Black-billed or **Cuban Whistling Duck** Dendrocygna arborea (L.) West Indies (Bahama Islands, Greater Antilles – Cuba, Haiti, Jamaica, Puerto Rico – Virgin Islands, Leeward Islands, Martinique).

9 Lesser or **Indian Whistling Duck** Dendrocygna javanica (HORSFIELD) India from Sind eastwards to coast of southern China, south to Sri lanka, Nicobar Islands, Malay Peninsular, Thailand, Cochin China; Riu Kiu Islands, south-western Borneo, Sumatra and Java.

10 White-faced Whistling Duck Dendrocygna viduata (L.) Tropical South America, south to the Argentine Chaco, Paraguay and Uruguay. Africa, south of the Sahara to southern Angola and the Transvaal; Madagascar; Comoros Islands.

11 Northern Red-billed Whistling Duck Dendrocygna autumnalis autumnalis (L.) Extreme southern Texas and Mexico, south throughout Central America to Panama, where it intergrades with *D.a. discolor*.

12 Southern Red-billed Whistling Duck Dendrocygna autumnalis discolor SCLATER & SALVIN South America from eastern Panama to northern Argentina, but not south of Ecuador on the west side of the Andes.

11

The two races 11
and 12 intergrade

12

1

Male has higher crown than
female

♂ and ♀ have the same plumage in
all the forms on this page

8

9

4

Medium

6

Small

5

Large

7

10

3

2

P.S.

PLATE 2 SWANS

Tribe Anserini

1 **Coscoroba Swan** *Coscoroba coscoroba* (MOLINA) Breeds in southern Brazil, Uruguay, Paraguay, Argentina, Chile (including Tierra del Fuego), and, possibly, Falkland Islands. Winters further north, to about 25ºS. This species may more properly belong to the Tribe *Dendrocygnini.*

2 **Black Swan** *Cygnus atratus* (LATHAM) Australia, on mainland (except north central) and Tasmania. Introduced into New Zealand, where now widespread.

3 ***Mute Swan** *Cygnus olor* (GMELIN) Now breeds wild in British Isles, north west Europe, Russia, Asia Minor and Iran, east through Turkestan to Mongolia. In winter to Black Sea, north-western India and Korea. Elsewhere widely introduced.

4 **Black-necked Swan** *Cygnus melanocoryphus* (MOLINA) Breeds in South America, from 30°S in Brazil, Paraguay, Uruguay, Falkland Islands, Argentina and Chile, south to Tierra del Fuego. In winter north to Tropic of Capricorn.

5 **Whistling Swan** *Cygnus columbianus columbianus* (ORD) North America, breeding chiefly north of Arctic Circle from Alaska to Hudson Bay, and wintering on the Atlantic coast from Chesapeake Bay to Currituck Sound and the Pacific coast from southern Alaska to California.

6 ***Bewick's Swan** *Cygnus columbianus bewickii* YARRELL Breeds in northern Russia from the Kanin peninsula and northern Siberia, east to the delta of Kolyma. South in Winter to Britain and Ireland and north-western Europe, the Caspian Sea, and Japan and China. Jankowski's Swan **(7)** , formerly regarded as a separate race on the basis of a larger, more yellow bill, is no longer considered as distinct from *C. c. bewickii.*

8 ***Whooper Swan** *Cygnus cygnus cygnus* (L.) Breeds from Iceland and northern Scandinavia eastwards to Kamchatka, Commander Islands and Japan. Winters in British Isles, western Europe, Asia Minor, northern India, central Asia, China and Japan. Seems formerly to have bred in Greenland, where frequently seen.

9 **Trumpeter Swan** *Cygnus cygnus buccinator* RICHARDSON Formerly bred throughout North America. Now known to breed only in Alberta, British Columbia, Montana, Wyoming and interior of Alaska. Population showing a welcome increase in recent years.

In the Swans the plumage of the
male and female (cob and pen)
is the same
Immatures are greyish with pale
flesh-coloured to orange bills

9

5

8

6

7

The two races **6**
and **7** intergrade

9

8

5

6

3

Adult and immature
The species which has become
largely domesticated

3

1

4

2

P.S.

PLATE 3 GREY GEESE

1 **Swan Goose** *Anser cygnoides* (L.) Breeds in southern Siberia, northern Mongolia and central Manchuria from the Tobol and the Ob to the Sea of Okhotsk and Sakhalin. Winters in China. Domestic varieties of "Chinese Geese" are derived from this species.

2 ***Western or Yellow-billed Bean Goose** *Anser fabalis fabalis* (LATHAM) Breeds in wooded country of the Arctic from Lapland eastwards to the Ural Mountains. Winters in Britain (now very local), Holland, Europe south to Mediterranean and Black Seas. Limits of ranges of this and next four races not yet fully determined.

3 **Johansen's Bean Goose** *Anser fabalis johanseni* DELACOUR Breeds in forested western Siberia east to Khatanga and south to about 61°N. Mingles and interbreeds with *rossicus* in the north and intergrades with *fabalis* and *middendorfi* where their ranges are in contact. Winters in Iran, Turkestan and western China.

4 **Middendorf's Bean Goose** *Anser fabalis middendorfi* SEVERTZOW Breeds in forests of eastern Siberia from the Khatanga to the Kolyma, south to the Altai. Winters in eastern China, northern Mongolia and Japan.

5 ***Russian Bean Goose** *Anser fabalis rossicus* BUTURLIN Breeds in Novaya Zemlya and on tundra shores of Arctic Russia and Siberia west of the Taimyr Peninsula. Winters in Europe west to Belgium and Holland, south to Italy; in southern Russia, Siberia, Turkestan and China. Individuals stray to Britain. "Sushkin's Goose" appears to be a colour phase of this race, with pink bill and legs.

6 **Thick-billed or Eastern Bean Goose** *Anser fabalis serrirostris* SWINHOE Breeds on the tundra shores of Siberia, east of the Yenesei. Winters in China and Japan.

7 ***Pink-footed Goose** *Anser brachyrhynchus* BAILLON Breeds in east Greenland, Iceland and Spitzbergen. Birds from Greenland and Iceland winter in Scotland and England, those from Spitzbergen in Denmark, Germany, Holland, Belgium, occasionally France.

8 ***European White-fronted Goose** *Anser albifrons albifrons* (SCOPOLI) Breeds on the Arctic coasts of Europe and Asia, east from the Kanin Peninsula, Kolguev and southern Novaya Zemlya to the Kolyma River and perhaps beyond. Winters in England and Wales, western Europe, and on shores of Mediterranean, Black and Caspian Seas.

9 **Pacific White-fronted Goose** *Anser albifrons frontalis* BAIRD Breeds in Arctic America, from Mackenzie River west to Bering Sea, and in eastern Siberia, but western limits unknown. Winters in western United States, south to Mexico and east to Louisiana; and in China and Japan.

10 ***Greenland White-fronted Goose** *Anser albifrons flavirostris* DALGETY AND SCOTT Breeds in west Greenland. Winters in Ireland, west Scotland, Wales, England (in small numbers); occasional in eastern North America.

11 **Tule Goose** *Anser albifrons gambelli* HARTLAUB Breeds taiga zone of north-west Canada and adjacent Alaska. Winters in Mexico and neighbouring states of the U.S.A., eg. Texas. Birds breeding in south-west Alaska, within taiga zone, and wintering exclusively within Sacramento Valley of California, have been identified as a separate race, Elgas's Goose, *A. a. elgasi*.

12 ***Lesser White-fronted Goose** *Anser erythropus* (L.) Breeds, mostly near mountain tarns, from Norwegian Lapland to the Kolyma in Siberia and perhaps farther eastwards. Winters in south-eastern Europe, Black and Caspian Seas, Turkestan, north-west India, China and Japan. Rare straggler to Britain, occurring almost annually in flocks of White-fronted or Bean Geese.

13 ***Western Greylag Goose** *Anser anser anser* (L.) Breeds in Scotland, though now only in small numbers, The only indigenous species of goose breeding in Britain. Breeding range includes Iceland, Scandinavia, east to Austria, Yugoslavia, Macedonia and the Caucasus. Winters in Britain, Holland, France, Spain, North Africa. Populations of western Russia and the Balkans are intermediate between this and the Eastern form and further study may reveal more distinguishable populations. The Greylag is the ancestor of domestic geese, other than Chinese.

14 **Eastern Greylag Goose** *Anser anser rubrirostris* SWINHOE Breeds eastwards from about 40°E and south of 60°N through Asia Minor and central Asia to Kamchatka. In winter to the eastern Mediterranean, Black and Caspian Seas and in Seistan, north-west India and China.

The plumage of males and females is the same

Domestic Chinese Goose

1 Ancestor of the domestic form

The races of Bean Goose all intergrade

7

5

3

6

2

4

9

11

10

8 Adult

8 Immature

Black belly markings of adult Whitefronts vary individually within wide limits

Domestic Embden Goose Drawn to smaller scale

12

13 Ancestor of domestic farmyard geese; e.g. Toulouse, Embden, Roman, Sebastopol, etc.

14

P.S.

PLATE 4 SNOW GEESE, ETC. (ABERRANT GREY GEESE)

1 **Bar-headed Goose** *Anser indicus* LATHAM
Breeds on lakes of high central Asia from the
Tian-Shans to Ladakh and Kokonor. Winters
northern India, Assam and northern Burma.

2 **Emperor Goose** *Anser canagicus*
SEWASTIANOW Breeds on the north-west coast of
Alaska from Kotzebue Sound to the Yukon
and Kuskokwim Rivers, on St. Lawrence
Island and in Siberia from the Anadyr along
the Chuckchi Peninsula. Winters in the
Aleutian Islands and the Alaska Peninsula, east
to Bristol Bay; in Asia, south to the
Commander Islands and Kamchatka.

3 ***Lesser Snow Goose** and **Blue Goose**
Anser caerulescens caerulescens (L.) Breeds on
Baffin and Southampton Islands and Arctic
coast of North America from Hudson's Bay
westward and in north-eastern Siberia,
probably as far west as the Lena. The Blue
Goose, formerly regarded as a distinct species,
now known to be a colour phase most
numerous at the eastern end of the range, but
spreading westwards and becoming more
numerous. Nearly all Blue Geese winter on the
coast of the Gulf of Mexico, chiefly in
Louisiana. Birds of the white phase
predominate in California, though some are
found on the Gulf coast. In Asia the race
occurs south to Japan, but the Siberian
population probably winters in America.
Individuals of both types have occurred as
stragglers in Britain, but some of those
recorded may have been escapes from
captivity.

4 ***Greater Snow Goose** *Anser caerulescens
atlanticus* KENNARD Breeds on the coast of
north-west Greenland, Ellesmere Land and
the adjacent islands. Migrates by way of Cap
Tourmente at mouth of St. Lawrence to winter
off Atlantic coast of U.S.A. from Chesapeake
Bay to North Carolina. A straggler to Britain,
though it is difficult to establish whether
records refer to wild birds or to escapes from
captivity in this country or elsewhere in
Europe.

5 **Ross's Goose** *Anser rossii* CASSIN Breeds in
the Perry River region in the centre of the
Arctic coast of Canada. The nest was first
found in 1940. Winters in Sacramento and
San Joaquin valleys in California. Total
population now substantially larger than
recorded formerly.

2

5

This race has no
blue phase

4

3

White phase
Immature

3

Blue phase
Immature

3

Blue phase
Adult White-breasted form

3

Blue phase
Typical adult

3

White phase
Adult

These are two colour phases
of the same sub-species

4

3

5

1

The plumage of males and females is the same

P.S.

PLATE 5 BLACK GEESE

1 *Atlantic Canada Goose Branta canadensis canadensis (L.) Breeds in south-east Baffin Island, Newfoundland, Labrador east of the Height of Land, and on Magdalen Islands. Winters on Atlantic coast from Nova Scotia south to Florida. Introduced into England first in seventeenth century and now generally regarded as British bird. Also introduced elsewhere in Europe and in New Zealand.

2 Central or **Todd's Canada Goose** Branta canadensis interior TODD Breeds in northern Quebec, Ontario, Manitoba, around southern Hudson Bay and James Bay. Winters from southern Ontario, Wisconsin, Illinois and Chesapeake Bay, along Atlantic coast south to Florida and Louisiana.

3 Great Basin or **Moffitt's Canada Goose** Branta canadensis moffitti ALDRICH Breeds from central British Columbia, Alberta and Saskatchewan to north-eastern California, northern Utah, northern Colorado and South Dakota. This race does not move far on migration but has been recorded in winter from southern British Columbia, north-western Wyoming and Arkansas, south to California and the Gulf of Mexico.

4 Giant Canada Goose Branta canadensis maxima DELACOUR Breeds western U.S.A. and south-west Canada, winters south-western U.S.A.

5 Lesser Canada Goose Branta canadensis parvipes (CASSIN) Breeds throughout the interior of northern North America from central Alaska east to Hudson Bay and south to northern British Columbia and Manitoba, where it intergrades with moffitti and interior. Breeds also on Baffin and Southampton Islands. Migrates mainly west of the Mississippi and winters in southern U.S. from California to Louisiana and south to Mexico.

6 Taverner's Canada Goose Branta canadensis taverneri DELACOUR Breeds in north-west interior from Alaska peninsula to the Perry River, where it intergrades with parvipes. Winters from Washington to Texas and Mexico, mainly in California. Also intergrades with occidentalis.

7 Dusky Canada Goose Branta canadensis occidentalis (BAIRD) Breeds around Prince William Sound and perhaps farther south along Gulf of Alaska. Winters within range and south to British Columbia and Oregon.

8 Vancouver Canada Goose Branta canadensis fulva DELACOUR Breeds along coast and on islands of British Columbia and southern Alaska. Largely non-migratory but wanderers have been found in northern California in winter.

9 Aleutian Canada Goose Branta canadensis leucopareia (BRANDT) Breeds Aleutian Islands, winters California. Increasing due to protection in winter.

10 Richardson's Canada Goose Branta canadensis hutchinsii (RICHARDSON) Breeds on Melville Peninsula, Southampton, Baffin and Ellesmere Islands. Migrates between Mississippi and Rocky Mountains to winter in Texas and Mexico.

11 Cackling Canada Goose Branta canadensis minima RIDGWAY Breeds along western shores of Alaska. Winters from southern British Columbia to southern California, in large interior valleys.

12 †Bering Canada Goose Branta canadensis asiatica ALDRICH Extinct. Bred Bering Island (Commander Islands) and Kurile Islands, until about 1900.

13 Hawaiian Goose or **Ne-ne** Branta sandvicensis (VIGORS) Breeds on main island of Hawaii. Recently reintroduced on Maui and Kauai, where has bred. Probably less than 50 left in 1947. About 500 now alive in Hawaii, many more in captivity.

14 *Barnacle Goose Branta leucopsis (BECHSTEIN) Three discrete populations: breeds east Greenland, winters west Scotland and Ireland; breeds Spitzbergen, winters Solway Firth, Scotland; breeds Novaya Zemlya and west Siberian Islands and also islands in Baltic, winters Holland.

15 *Russian or **Dark-bellied Brent Goose** Branta bernicla bernicla (L.) Breeds in Arctic Europe and Asia from Kolguev east to Severnaya Zemlya, mainly on Taimyr Peninsula. Winters on coasts of England and north-west Europe.

16 *Atlantic or **Light-bellied Brent Goose** Branta bernicla hrota (O. F. MÜLLER) Breeds on coasts and islands of eastern Arctic Canada, northern Greenland, Spitzbergen, Franz Joseph Land. Winters in Ireland, and erratically elsewhere on coasts of north-west Europe, and on Atlantic coast of U.S.A. from New Jersey to North Carolina.

17 Lawrence's Brent Goose Branta bernicla orientalis (LAWRENCE) Breeding area unknown, probably north-east of Hudson's Bay. Winters on coast of New Jersey. Very rare, possibly never existed as a distinct race.

18 *Pacific Brent Goose or **Black Brant** Branta bernicla nigricans TOUGARINOV Breeds on coasts and islands of western Arctic Canada, northern Alaska and Siberia, west to Taimyr Peninsula. Winters on shores of the Pacific south to Japan and northern China and from Vancouver Island to Lower California, principally in U.S.A. Occasional records of this race in Britain.

19 *Red-breasted Goose Branta ruficollis (PALLAS) Breeds on the Siberian tundra from the Ob to the Khatanga. Winters in southern part of the Caspian Sea and in the Aral Sea. Scarce in Europe, straggler in Britain.

12
Extinct

9
Apparent tendency
to white ring

11
Small and dark

10
Small and pale

6

5

4

7

8

3

2

1

17

18
Ring complete
in front

15

16

13

14

19

In all these forms the plumage of
both sexes is the same

P.S.

PLATE 6 SHELDUCKS AND SHELDGEESE

Sub-Family **Anatinae**

Tribe **Tadornini**

I †Crested Shelduck *Tadorna cristata* (KURODA) Known only from three specimens, two from Korea and one from near Vladivostok. Thought at first to be a hybrid, but figures fairly frequently in ancient Japanese prints, indicating that it is probably a recently extinct species.

2 *Ruddy Shelduck *Tadorna ferruginea* (PALLAS) Breeds in south Spain and from south-east Europe, the Near East, the Caspian Sea, across Asia to Transbaikalia, south to Himalayas and south-western China. Winters in southern half of its breeding range to the Nile Valley; India and southern China. Occasional in Britain.

3 South African or **Cape Shelduck** *Tadorna cana* (GMELIN) Cape Province, Orange Free State and Transvaal, north to Namibia and Botswana.

4 Australian Shelduck *Tadorna tadornoides* (JARDINE AND SELBY) Very numerous in southern South Australia and Victoria and in Tasmania; a straggler further north.

5 Paradise or **New Zealand Shelduck** *Tadorna variegata* (GMELIN) Widespread in North, South and Stewart Islands, New Zealand.

6 Moluccan or **Black-backed Radjah Shelduck** *Tadorna radjah radjah* (LESSON) Moluccas, Ceram, Buru, Waigiu. Salawati, New Guinea and the Aru Islands.

7 Australian or **Red-backed Radjah Shelduck** or **Burdekin Duck** *Tadorna radjah rufitergum* HARTERT Northern and eastern tropical Australia.

8 *Common Shelduck *Tadorna tadorna* (L.) Breeds on coasts of western Europe, including the British Isles; locally about the shores of the Mediterranean, Black and Caspian Seas, east on the saline lakes of central Asia to east Siberia, Mongolia and Tibet. Winters from southern part of its breeding range to northern Africa, Arabia, India, south China and Japan.

9 Egyptian Goose *Alopochen aegyptiacus* (L.) Africa, south of the Sahara, also the entire Nile Valley. Occasional records in Europe. Introduced into England, but feral stock remains small.

10 Orinoco Goose *Neochen jubatus* (SPIX) Basins of the Orinoco and the Amazon.

8

♀ ♂

1
Now extinct

Slightly smaller

6 ♂

♂

7 ♂

♂ & ♀ the same
in both races

2 ♀ ♂

3 ♀ ♂

4 ♀ ♂

5 ♀ ♂

10

♂ & ♀ plumage
the same

9

♂ & ♀ the same

There are two colour
phases, the second
being greyer on the
back than this one

P.S.

PLATE 7 SHELDGEESE

1 Abyssinian Blue-winged Goose *Cyanochen cyanopterus* (RÜPPELL) Highlands of Ethiopia.

2 Andean Goose *Chloephaga melanoptera* (EYTON) Western South America from the highlands of Peru and Bolivia to the Straits of Magellan. In winter it descends to the plains at the foot of the Andes in Chile and Argentina.

3 Ashy-headed Goose *Chloephaga poliocephala* SCLATER Southern Chile and Argentina, Tierra del Fuego; Falkland Islands (rare). Migrates north in winter, but limits of breeding and winter ranges not clearly established.

4 Ruddy-headed Goose *Chloephaga rubidiceps* SCLATER Falkland Islands and Tierra del Fuego; occasional in Patagonia and central Argentina. Northward movements in winter not yet worked out.

5 Upland or **Lesser Magellan Goose** *Chloephaga picta picta* (GMELIN) Chile and southern Argentina from the Rio Negro south to Tierra del Fuego. In this form the males may be barred or white-breasted; the barred form predominates near the coast and to the south, the white form inland and to the north.

6 Falkland Upland or **Greater Magellan Goose** *Chloephaga picta leucoptera* (GMELIN) Falkland Islands. Introduced into South Georgia. Larger than the typical form and males are always white-breasted.

7 Patagonian or **Lesser Kelp Goose** *Chloephaga hybrida hybrida* (MOLINA) Coast of Chile from Chiloë, southward to Tierra del Fuego.

8 Falkland or **Greater Kelp Goose** *Chloephaga hybrida malvinarum* PHILLIPS Falkland Islands.

All on this page except the Abyssinian are South American

1

Male and female plumage the same

2

Male and female plumage the same

6 ♀

♂ White form

♂

Males are never barred in this form

♀

♂ Barred form

5

3 ♂ and ♀ the same

4 ♂ and ♀ the same

7 ♀

♂

Local race with longer bill and legs

8 ♀ ♂

P.S.

PLATE 8

Aberrant species with affinities to tribe
Tadornini

I Cereopsis or **Cape Barren Goose**
Cereopsis novae-hollandiae LATHAM Islands off southern coast of Western Australia, South Australia and in Bass Strait. This species should probably be placed in a monotypic tribe, Cereopsini, close to the Anserini.

2 Flying Steamer Duck *Tachyeres patachonicus* (KING) Coasts, rivers, and interior lakes of southern South America from Valdivia, Chile on the west and Puerto Deseado, Argentina, on the east, south to Tierra del Fuego; Falklands Islands.

3 Magellanic Flightless Steamer Duck
Tachyeres pteneres (FORSTER) The coast of southern South America from Concepción, Chile, south to Tierra del Fuego, including the Straits of Magellan to the eastern entrance, but not the Atlantic coasts north of Cape San Diego.

4 Falkland Island Flightless Steamer Duck *Tachyeres brachypterus* (LATHAM) Falkland Islands.

White-headed Flightless Steamer Duck *Tachyeres leucocephalus* (HUMPHREY AND THOMPSON) Chubut Province, southern Argentina. This species (not illustrated) was first described in 1981. It has more white on the head at all times of year than other steamer ducks.

Steamer Ducks should probably be placed in a separate tribe, Tachyerini, since their relationship to other ducks remains obscure.

5 Patagonian Crested Duck *Lophonetta specularioides specularioides* (KING) From central Chile and west central Argentina south to Tierra del Fuego; Falkland Islands.

6 Andean Crested Duck *Lophonetta specularioides alticola* MÉNÉGAUX Highland lakes in the Andes from central Peru, south through Bolivia to the latitude of Santiago, Chile. Occasionally in winter to the central valley of Chile.

Crested Ducks are probably more closely related to the Anatini (Dabbling Ducks) than to the Shelducks.

Larger, with buff chin

♀ ♂

6

Smaller, with white chin and mottled belly

♀ ♂

5

Magellanic Steamer is largest, coarsest, palest. Has less red on throat

♀ ♂

3

These Crested Ducks are probably more closely related to the Bronze-winged Ducks than to the Shelducks

♀ ♂

4

Flying Steamer is darker and smaller than the other two

♀ ♂

2

1

♂ and ♀ the same

P.S.

PLATE 9 DABBLING DUCKS

Tribe **Anatini**

1 **Marbled Teal** Marmaronetta (Anas) angustirostris (MÉNÉTRIÈS) Resident in Mediterranean Basin from southern Spain to Near East, Iran, Baluchistan and north-western India.

2 **Bronze-winged Duck** Anas specularis KING Slopes of the Andes in Chile and Argentina from the latitude of Concepción to Tierra del Fuego. North in winter to the vicinity of Valparaíso, Chile.

3 **Salvadori's Duck** Anas waigiuensis (ROTHS-CHILD AND HARTERT) Mountains of New Guinea.

4 **Cape Teal** Anas capensis GMELIN Africa from Botswana, African lakes, Uganda and southern Ethiopia southward. Apparently not in eastern coastal areas. Recorded from Lake Chad and Senegambia.

5 **Hottentot Teal** Anas hottentota EYTON Africa from Angola, Uganda and Shoa to Cape Province; Madagascar. Recently found in Chad.

6 **Northern Silver** or **Versicolor Teal** Anas versicolor versicolor VIEILLOT South America from central Chile, the Bolivian Chaco, Paraguay and southern Brazil, south to central Argentina.

7 **Southern Silver** or **Versicolor Teal** Anas versicolor fretensis KING South America from the latitude of Valdivia, Chile, through southern Chile and Argentina to Tierra del Fuego; Falkland Islands.

8 **Puna Teal** Anas versicolor puna TSCHUDI Puna (highland plateau) of the Andes from central Peru, south through Bolivia (Lake Titicaca and Cochabamba) to northern Chile.

9 **Red-billed Pintail** Anas erythrorhyncha GMELIN South and East Africa from southern Angola, Lakes Tanganyika and Victoria and southern Ethiopia, south to the Cape; Madagascar.

10 **Lesser** or **Nothern Bahama Pintail** Anas bahamensis bahamensis L. Bahama Islands, Greater Antilles (Cuba, Haiti, Jamaica, Puerto Rico) northern Lesser Antilles, northern Colombia, the Guianas and northern Brazil, as far as Amazon.

11 **Greater** or **Southern Bahama Pintail** Anas bahamensis rubrirostris VIEILLOT Southern Brazil, Paraguay, Uruguay, south to northern and eastern Argentina, and west to eastern Bolivia; central provinces of Chile; recorded on west coast of Peru.

12 **Galapagos Pintail** Anas bahamensis galapagensis RIDGWAY Galapagos Islands (Pacific Ocean west of Ecuador).

13 **South Georgian Teal** Anas georgica georgica GMELIN Island of South Georgia (South Atlantic).

14 **Chilean** or **Brown Pintail** Anas georgica spinicauda VIEILLOT South America from southern Colombia and Ecuador, through Bolivia, southern Brazil, Paraguay, Uruguay, Argentina and Chile to Tierra del Fuego; Falkland Islands. Probably does not winter in extreme south of its range.

15 **†Niceforo's Pintail** Anas georgica niceforoi WETMORE AND BORRERO Eastern Andes of Colombia; also Cali, Valle de Cauca, Colombia. Now extinct.

16 ***Northern Pintail** Anas acuta acuta L. Breeds in the northern parts of Europe, Asia and North America, including British Isles. Winters south to North Africa, the Nile Valley, Ethiopia, Persian Gulf, India, Sri Lanka, Burma, Thailand, southern China; from southern British Columbia, Mississippi Valley and Chesapeake Bay to Panama and West Indies; Hawaiian Islands.

17 **Kerguelen** or **Eaton's Pintail** Anas acuta eatoni (SHARPE) Kerguelen Island. Recently introduced into St. Paul and Amsterdam Islands (all in South Indian Ocean).

18 **Crozet Pintail** Anas acuta drygalskii REICHENOW Crozet Islands (South Indian Ocean, 800 miles west of Kerguelen Island).

19 **Chilean Teal** Anas flavirostris flavirostris VIEILLOT South America from central Chile, north-western Argentina and extreme southern Brazil, south to Tierra del Fuego; Falkland Islands.

20 **Sharp-winged Teal** Anas flavirostris oxyptera MEYER The Puna zone (highland plateau) of the Andes from northern Peru, south through western Bolivia to northern Chile and northern Argentina.

21 **Andean Teal** Anas flavirostris andium (SCLATER AND SALVIN) High Andes of central and southern Colombia and of Ecuador.

22 **Merida Teal** Anas flavirostris altipetens (CONOVER) High Andes of western Venezuela and the eastern Andes of Colombia, south to Bogota.

23 ***European Green-winged Teal** Anas crecca crecca L. Breeds in Europe and Asia from Iceland to China, Manchuria and Kurile Islands and Japan. Winters as far south as North Africa, Nile Valley, Somalia, Iran, India and Sri Lanka, Assam, southern China and the Philippines.

24 **Aleutian Teal** Anas crecca nimia FRIEDMANN Aleutian Islands.

25 ***American Green-winged Teal** Anas crecca carolinensis GMELIN Breeds in northern North America from Alaska to Hudson Bay south to about 40°N. Winters in southern U.S.A., Mexico, northern Central America and the West Indies. Vagrant to Britain.

Except where shown these are all drakes. The females are duller

6 and 7 intergrade
10 and 11 intergrade

♀ ♂

♂ ♂

♀

Merida is a lighter version of Andean
♀♀ of these 4 are almost the same as ♂♂

♂ ♂

♀

P.S.

PLATE 10 DABBLING DUCKS

1 **Baikal** or **Formosa Teal** *Anas formosa*
GEORGI Breeds in Siberia east from the Yenisei
River to the Kolyma delta and Anadyr, south
to Lake Baikal, northern Sakhalin and
northern Kamchatka. Winters in China and
Japan. Recorded from Taiwan, formerly
Formosa, but derives its name not from the
island but from the fact that "formosa" is the
Latin for "beautiful".

2 **Falcated Teal** *Anas falcata* GEORGI Breeds in
northern Asia, south of the Arctic Circle from
the Upper Yenesei to Kamchatka, south to
Lake Baikal, northern Mongolia, the Amur
and Ussuriland. Winters in Japan, Korea,
eastern and southern China to Upper Burma.

3 **Madagascar Teal** *Anas bernieri* (HARTLAUB)
Western part of Madagascar. Believed to be
very rare.

4 **East Indian Grey Teal** *Anas gibberifrons
gibberifrons* S. MÜLLER Central Indonesia (Java,
Celebes, Lesser Sunda Islands, Sabeyer,
Sumba, Flores, Timor and Wetar).

5 †**Rennell Island Grey Teal** *Anas
gibberifrons remissa* RIPLEY Rennell Island.
Now extinct.

6 **Australian Grey Teal** *Anas gibberifrons
gracilis* BULLER Australia, New Zealand, New
Guinea, Aru and Kei Islands and New
Caledonia. A recent arrival in New Zealand,
where it has spread rapidly.

7 **Andaman Teal** *Anas gibberifrons albogularis*
(HUME) Andaman Islands, Landfall and Great
Coco Islands (Indian Ocean). Two races have
been described from the islands, but since
there is striking individual variation in this
species the claim of *A.a.leucopareus* is not
substantiated.

8 **Chestnut Teal** *Anas castanea* (EYTON)
Australia (except north coast); abundant in
Tasmania and southern Victoria.

9 **Auckland Island Teal** *Anas aucklandica
aucklandica* (G.R. GRAY) Auckland Islands (400
miles south of New Zealand). Lately reported
to be holding its own satisfactorily, though
now extinct on Auckland Island itself.

10 **Campbell Island Teal** *Anas aucklandica
nesiotis* (FLEMING) Campbell Island (500 miles
south of New Zealand). Very rare, on Dent
Island only.

11 **New Zealand Brown Teal** *Anas
aucklandica chlorotis* G.R. GRAY New Zealand.
Rare. Became extinct Chatham Islands about
1915.

♀

♂

Erythristic form
of Grey Teal

3

4

High forehead

5

Smallest of the three

6

♀

♂

8

♀

♂

7

Island form of Grey Teal
with variable amount of
white on face

11

♀

♂ Dull plumage

Many males
are intermediate
between these two

♂ Bright plumage

9

♀

♂

10

Narrower bill

P.S.

PLATE II DABBLING DUCKS (MALLARDS)

1 ***Mallard** *Anas platyrhynchos platyrhynchos* L. Breeds in Europe and Asia from Arctic Circle, south to Mediterranean, Iran, Tibet, central China, Korea and northern Japan; Iceland; the Azores; northern and central North America, west of Hudson's Bay and the Mississippi. Winters from southern half of breeding range to North Africa, Nile Valley, India, Burma, southern China, Japan; southern Mexico and Florida. Successfully introduced New Zealand.

2 **Greenland Mallard** *Anas platyrhynchos conboschas* C.L.BREHM Breeds on coasts of Greenland, on the west, north of Upernavik and on the east, north to Angmagssalik.

3 **Florida Duck** *Anas platyrhynchos fulvigula* RIDGWAY Resident southern Florida. Mottled Duck *A. p. maculosa* once again regarded as separate race, mainly resident Gulf coasts of U.S.A. and Mexico.

4 **Mexican Duck** *Anas platyrhynchos diazi* (RIDGWAY) Highlands of central Mexico and the upper Rio Grande Valley from El Paso, Texas to Albuquerque, New Mexico.

(Oustalets Duck from the islands of Guam, Saipan and Tinian, 1,200 miles north of New Guinea, was described as a distinct species, or at least race, *A. (platyrhynchos) oustaleti*, but research by Kuroda has shown this population to result from hybridisation of *A. platyrhynchos* and *A. superciliosa*.)

5 ***North American Black Duck** *Anas rubripes* BREWSTER Breeds in north-eastern North America from the west side of Hudson Bay to Labrador, and south to North Carolina. Winters south to the Gulf coast. Recorded very rarely in British Isles.

6 **Hawaiian Duck** *Anas wyvilliana* SCLATER Resident Kauai, reintroduced Oahu and Hawaii islands. Population has increased to c.2500 (1993).

7 **Laysan Teal** *Anas laysanensis* ROTHSCHILD Layson Island (900 miles west of Honolulu). Once very scarce (only 7 individuals left in 1912) but has recently increased substantially, fluctuating up to 700 birds.

8 **Indian Spotbill** *Ansa poecilorhyncha poecilorhyncha* FORSTER India to western Assam; Sri Lanka.

9 **Burma Spotbill** *Anas poecilorhyncha haringtoni* (OATES) Burma, Shan States, Yunnan.

10 **Chinese Spotbill** *Anas poecilorhyncha zonorhyncha* SWINHOE Breeds in eastern Siberia, Manchuria, Mongolia, northern China, Korea, southern Sakhalin, the Kurile Islands and Japan. Winters south to southern China and Taiwan.

11 **New Zealand Grey Duck** *Anas superciliosa superciliosa* GMELIN New Zealand and neighbouring islands.

12 **Pelew Island Grey Duck** *Anas superciliosa pelewensis* HARTLAUB AND FINSCH Pelew Islands (east of Philippine Islands), northern New Guinea, Solomon Islands, Fiji, Samona, Tonga, Tahiti, New Caledonia, New Hebrides, Bismarck Archipelago.

13 **Australian Black Duck** *Anas superciliosa rogersi* MATHEWS Australia and Tasmania, and much of Indonesia.

14 **Philippine Duck** *Anas luzonica* FRASER Philippine Islands.

15 **Meller's Duck** *Anas melleri* SCLATER Eastern half of Madagascar; introduced into Mauritius.

16 **African Yellowbill** *Anas undulata undulata* DU BOIS Africa from Angola, Uganda and Kenya southward.

17 **Abyssinian Yellowbill** *Anas undulata ruppelli* BLYTH Upper Blue Nile and Ethiopian Lake Region. Probably also Cameroon (one collected).

18 **African Black Duck** *Anas sparsa sparsa* EYTON South Africa; northern limits of range not yet known reliably, but as far as East Africa and Malawi.

19 **Abyssinian Black Duck** *Anas sparsa leucostigma* RÜPPELL Ethiopia, Sudan, East Africa across to the Upper Congo, and Tanzania. Rare in the western part of its range.

20 **Gabon Black Duck** *Anas sparsa maclatchyi* BERLIOZ Western Equatorial Africa. Probably not a valid race.

2

1 ♀

♂

Domestic Duck

Drawn to smaller scale

5

4

3

Black spot

8

9

10

Bill deeper yellow

Females mostly just duller edition of male

12 ♂

13 ♂

♂

16 ♂

♂

Darker

17

Smallest

11

Largest

Greyer

20

19 ♂

♂

These Black Ducks intergrade

14

Female similar to male

18

7

6

15

Females also show white round eye

Female like small female Mallard

P.S.

PLATE 12 DABBLING DUCKS

1 *Gadwall *Anas strepera strepera* L. Europe, Asia and western North America, breeding from Iceland to Kamchatka, British Columbia and Prairie Provinces of Canada, south to England, Holland, Germany, central Russia, Caspian, Siestan, Transbaikalia, California and Colorado. Winters south to northern Africa, Ethiopia, India, Assam, southern China, Lower California, southern Mexico and Florida.

2 †Coues's Gadwall *Anas strepera couesi* (STREETS) Washington Is., New York Is. (Fanning Group, 1,000 miles S. of Hawaii). Extinct.

3 *European Wigeon *Anas penelope* L. Europe and Asia, breeding in temperate regions north to the Arctic Circle and beyond, from Iceland and Scotland to Kamchatka. Winters in Britain and south to Nile Valley, Ethiopia, India, southern China and Japan. Regularly in small numbers on the Atlantic coasts of North America, also in British Columbia.

4 *American Wigeon *Anas americana* GMELIN North America, breeding in the north-west from Alaska to the Prairie Provinces, mainly east of the Rockies and wintering from British Columbia to California and the Gulf Coast, and from Long Island, south to Costa Rica and West Indies. Rare vagrant to Britain.

5 Chiloe Wigeon *Anas sibilatrix* POEPPIG Southern South America from Chile and southern Brazil, south to Tierra del Fuego; Falkland Islands. Breeds in the southern half of its range.

6 *Blue-winged Teal *Anas discors* L. Formerly thought to be separated into two races Prairie Blue-winged Teal *A. d. discors* (6) and Atlantic Blue-winged Teal *A. d. orphana* (7), but now considered to be just a single species. Breeds Canada and U.S.A. from southern Alaska to Newfoundland south to prairies, avoiding coasts except in north-east U.S.A. Winters from southern U.S.A., through Mexico, Central America and West Indies, to northern South America, south to northern Peru and northern Brazil. Occurs as a vagrant in Britain.

8 Argentine Cinnamon Teal *Anas cyanoptera cyanoptera* VIEILLOT Breeds in South America from southern Peru, Brazil and Uruguay south, and in Falkland Islands.

9 Andean Cinnamon Teal *Anas cyanoptera orinomus* (OBERHOLSER) Puna region (highland plateau) of the Andes in Peru, Bolivia and Chile.

10 Borrero's Cinnamon Teal *Anas cyanoptera borreroi* SNYDER AND LUMSDEN Breeds in highlands of Colombia. Exact limits of range not yet known.

11 Tropical Cinnamon Teal *Anas cyanoptera tropica* SNYDER AND LUMSDEN Lowlands of Colombia.

12 Northern Cinnamon Teal *Anas cyanoptera septentrionalium* SNYDER AND LUMSDEN Breeds in western North America from southern British Columbia to Mexico, east to Kansas and Texas. Winters south to Colombia and Venezuela.

13 *Garganey *Anas querquedula* L. Breeds in southern England, south Sweden, Finland, Russia, east across Asia, south of lat. 60°N. to Kamchatka; southern limits, France, Italy, Black Sea, Turkestan, Manchuria and northern Japan. Winters Africa south of the Sahara, south to Zambia, Indo-China, Philippines, Celebes, Moluccas and New Guinea.

14 Argentine Red Shoveler *Anas platalea* VIEILLOT Southern South America from Peru and Bolivia to southern Brazil and south to Tierra del Fuego and Falkland Islands; migratory in northern and southern parts of its range.

15 Cape or South African Shoveler *Anas smithi* (HARTERT) South Africa, north to Angola, Botswana and the Transvaal.

16 Australian Shoveler *Anas rhynchotis rhynchotis* LATHAM Main strongholds in south-east South Australia and south-west New South Wales.

17 New Zealand Shoveler *Anas rhynchotis variegata* (GOULD) New Zealand. Formerly Chatham Islands.

18 * Common Shoveler *Anas clypeata* L. Breeds in Europe, Asia and North America, not north of Arctic Circle nor in eastern Canada. Breeds commonly in Britain. Winters as far south as East Africa, Persian Gulf, Sri Lanka, Burma, southern China, Japan, Hawaii, Lower California, Mexico, Honduras, Florida.

PLATE 13

Aberrant species with affinities to the tribe

Anatini

1 Ringed Teal *Calonetta leucophrys* VIEILLOT South America from southern Bolivia, Paraguay, south-western and southern Brazil to north-eastern Argentina and Uruguay. The Ringed Teal is probably more nearly related to the Cairinini (Perching Ducks) than to the Anatini.

2 Blue or **Mountain Duck** *Hymenolaimus malacorhynchos* (GMELIN) Now confined to remote mountain streams of New Zealand. Formerly common, was confined to remote and relatively unmodified localities. This species has recently been split into two races, one on each main island. The North Island Blue Duck *H. m. hymenolaimus*, is resident in central North Island, while the South Island Blue Duck *H. m. malacoryhnchos*, is confined to the west of South Island

3 Pink-eared Duck *Malacorhynchus membranaceus* (LATHAM) Inland Australia. Highly nomadic and varies greatly in abundance, depending on rainfall.

4 †Pink-headed Duck *Rhodonessa caryophyllacea* (LATHAM) North-eastern and eastern India, Nepal and Assam, south to Madras. Was always local and rare, now probably extinct. No reliable reports of wild birds since 1935. Last in captivity died about 1939. Probably a member of the Aythyini (Pochards).

5 Freckled Duck *Stictonetta naevosa* (GOULD) The rarest of Australian ducks, perhaps dangerously so. Principal remaining breeding grounds are in South Australia, and are threatened by drainage. This species is possibly a member of the Anserini.

This species seems to be more closely related to the Perching Ducks than to the Dabbling Ducks

♀

♂

1

♀

♂

4

Probably now extinct

♀

♂

Male's bill is only red in breeding season

5

Soft flap at tip of bill

3

In both these species ♂ and ♀ are similar

2

P.S.

PLATE 14 TORRENT DUCKS

Tribe **Merganettini**

1 **Chilean Torrent Duck** *Merganetta armata armata* GOULD Andes of Chile and adjoining parts of western Argentina, north to Province of Mendoza, south to Tierra del Fuego.

2 **Colombian Torrent Duck** *Merganetta armata colombiana* DES MURS Andes of Venezuela, Colombia and northern Ecuador.

3 **Peruvian Torrent Duck** *Merganetta armata leucogenis* (TSCHUDI) Andes of central and southern Ecuador and of Peru (except for Tinta, the Cuzcan Andes and Rio Victor - occupied by *M.a. turneri*).

4 **Turner's Torrent Duck** *Merganetta armata turneri* SCLATER AND SALVIN Known only from Tinta, the Cuzcan Andes and Rio Victor (Dept. of Arequipa) Peru.

5 **Garlepp's** or **Bolivian Torrent Duck** *Merganetta armata garleppi* BERLEPSCH Mountains of Bolivia. Intergrades with *turneri* in the north and *berlepschi* in the south.

6 **Berlepsch's** or **Argentine Torrent Duck** *Merganetta armata berlepschi* HARTERT Mountains of north-western Argentina (Provinces of Salta and Tucumàn).

Recent work indicates that the last three sub-species are probably no more than variants of *M.a. leucogenis*.

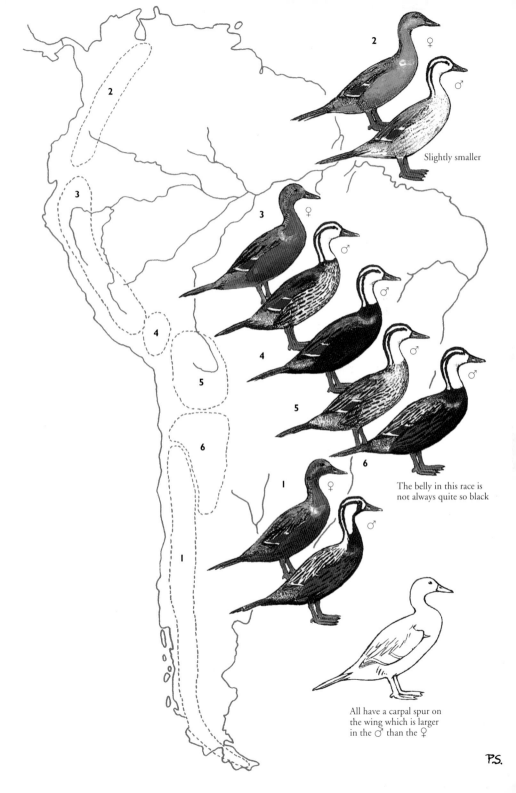

2 ♀
♂
Slightly smaller

3 ♀
♂

4 ♂

5 ♂

6 ♂

The belly in this race is
not always quite so black

1 ♀
♂

All have a carpal spur on
the wing which is larger
in the ♂ than the ♀

P.S.

PLATE 15 EIDERS

Tribe **Somateriini**

1 ***European Eider** *Somateria mollissima mollissima* (L.) Breeds in Iceland, British Isles, Scandinavia, east to Novaya Zemlya. Mainly resident but some winter in North Sea and on west coast of France.

2 **Pacific Eider** *Somateria mollissima v-nigra* G.R. GRAY Breeds on Arctic coasts and islands of north-eastern Asia, Commander and Aleutian Islands and coasts of Alaska and North-West Territories of Canada. Winters chiefly in the Aleutian Islands.

3 **Northern Eider** *Somateria mollissima borealis* (C.L. BREHM) Breeds on north-eastern coasts of Canada and west Greenland. Winters from the open waters of Greenland, south to Maine.

4 **American Eider** *Somateria mollissima dresseri* SHARPE Breeds Labrador to Maine. Winters within and to south of range.

Hudson Bay Eider *Somateria mollissima sedentaria* SNYDER Resident in Hudson Bay (not illustrated).

5 **Faeroe Eider** *Somateria mollissima faeroeensis* C.L. BREHM Faeroes; resident.

6 ***King Eider** *Somateria spectabilis* (L.) Breeds on fresh water near the Arctic coasts and on islands of Europe, Asia, and North America. Rare straggler to the British Isles in winter.

7 **Spectacled** or **Fischer's Eider** *Somateria fischeri* (BRANDT) Breeds on the New Siberian Islands and Arctic coast of Siberia from the Yana River to Bering Strait and on the coast of Alaska. Probably winters in the Bering Sea north of the Aleutian Islands, but range uncertain.

8 ***Steller's Eider** *Polysticta stelleri* (PALLAS) Breeds on the Arctic coast of Siberia from the Taimyr Peninsula to Bering Strait and the coast of Alaska. Winters on open waters of Kamchatka, Commander and Kurile Islands, Aleutian Islands and Kenai Peninsula (Alaska), and in Norwegian fjords and Baltic Sea. Rarely recorded in Britain.

The eiders are included in the tribe Mergini by some authorities.

2 Largest

♀

3

Medium sized

First year drakes have only patchy white breast and back

♂

♀

♀

♂

Smallest

♂

5

4 Medium

♀

2

♀

♂

♂

♀

Large

3

4

1

1

5

♀

7

♂

6

♂

♀

6

♂

7

8

♀

♂

P.S.

PLATE 16 POCHARDS

Tribe **Aythyini**

1 ***Red-crested Pochard** *Netta rufina* (PALLAS) Eastern Europe and Asia, breeding from southern France, Holland (few), through lower Danube, southern Russia west across Kirghiz Steppes to west Siberia. Winters Mediterranean, India, Burma, Shan States to China. Scarce vagrant to Britain; small numbers of escaped birds breed.

2 **Rosybill** *Netta peposaca* (VIEILLOT) Central Chile, south to Chiloë Island, east across Argentina to Paraguay, Uruguay and south to northern Patagonia.

3 **South American Pochard** *Netta erythrophthalma erythrophthalma* (WIED) Western South America from north-western Venezuela to southern Peru.

4 **African Pochard** *Netta erythrophthalma brunnea* (EYTON) Africa from Angola in the west to Ethiopia and south to Cape Province.

5 **Canvasback** *Aythya valisineria* (WILSON) North America, breeding in western Prairie Provinces of Canada and west central United States. Wintering from British Columbia, Colorado, southern Illinois and Chesapeake Bay, south to California, central Mexico, the Gulf and Florida.

6 ***European Pochard** *Aythya ferina* (L.) Breeds in British Isles, southern Scandinavia and central Russia through west Siberia to Lake Baikal, south to Holland, Germany, Balkans, Black Sea, Kirghiz Steppes and Yarkand. Winters in breeding range and south to Nile Valley, India, Burma and south China.

7 ***Redhead** *Aythya americana* (EYTON) Breeds in western North America. Winters in U.S. and south to Lower California and the Valley of Mexico.

2
♀
♂

1
♀
♂

3
Slightly smaller
and darker
♀
♂

4
Larger, paler
♂

Female similar to
female South
American Pochard

5
♀
♂

To distinguish these three,
note shape of head, and,
in the males, the colour of
the back and of the eye

6
♀
♂

7
♀
♂

Round head

P.S.

PLATE 17 POCHARDS

1 †**Madagascar White-eye** *Aythya innotata* (SALVADORI) Northern and eastern Madagascar. Probably extinct; not seen since 1991.

2 ****Common White-eye** or **Ferruginous Duck** *Aythya nyroca* (GÜLDENSTÄDT) Breeds in southern Europe, Balkans, Poland and west Siberia to the Ob Valley, south to northern Africa, Iran, Turkestan, Kashmir, the Pamirs and southern Tibet. Winters in the Mediterranean, Nile Valley, Persian Gulf, India and Burma. Rare vagrant to Britain.

3 **Baer's Pochard** *Aythya baeri* (RADDE) Breeds from Transbaikalia to the lower Ussuri and the Amur. Winters in China, Korea, Japan, upper Assam and Burma.

4 **Australian White-eye** or **Hardhead** *Aythya australis australis* (EYTON) Australia, New Guinea, New Caledonia, casual in Indonesia. Has occurred in New Zealand.

5 **Bank's Island White-eye** *Aythya australis extima* MAYR Banks and Gaua Islands (north of New Hebrides). May not be separate race.

6 **New Zealand Scaup** or **Black Teal** *Aythya novae-seelandiae* (GMELIN) New Zealand, Auckland Islands, Chatham Islands.

7 ****Ring-necked Duck** *Aythya collaris* (DONOVAN) Breeds in central and north-western North America. Winters in southern U.S., south to Guatemala and West Indies. Accidental in Britain.

8 ****Tufted Duck** *Aythya fuligula* (L.) Breeds in Europe and Asia from Iceland and British Isles to the Commander Islands (Pacific), south to central Europe, Balkans, Kirghiz Steppes, Lake Baikal, the Amur and Sakhalin. Winters in southern half of breeding range and south to Nile Valley, Persian Gulf, India, south China and Philippines.

9 ****Lesser Scaup** *Aythya affinis* (EYTON) Breeds in north-central and north-western Canada and U.S. Winters in southern U.S., south to Panama and West Indies.

10 ****European Greater Scaup** *Aythya marila marila* (L.) Breeds in northern Europe and Asia, east to the Lena. Has bred Scotland. Winters on coasts of western Europe (including Britain), eastern Mediterranean, Black Sea, Persian Gulf, north-western India.

11 **Pacific Greater Scaup** *Aythya marila mariloides* (VIGORS) Breeds in North America from Hudson's Bay to the Aleutians, Bering Island, Kamchatka and probably elsewhere on the eastern Asiatic mainland. Winters on Pacific and Atlantic coasts of North America, south to Lower California and the West Indies, also China, Korea and Japan.

2

3

♀

♂

5

Smaller, but perhaps
not a separate race

1

♀

♂

Some females
have white under
tail, especially in
autumn

♀

♂

4

7

♀

♂

♀

♂

8

♀

♂

6

9

♀

♂

Female in summer

♀

♀

♂

♀

♂

10

11

Slightly smaller and darker on back

P.S.

PLATE 18 PERCHING DUCKS

Tribe **Cairinini**
(Wood Ducks or Perching Ducks and Geese)

1 **Lesser Brazilian Teal** *Amazonetta brasiliensis brasiliensis* (GMELIN) Eastern South America from the Orinoco, western Brazil, eastern Bolivia, Paraguay, Uruguay and northern Argentina. There is a light and dark colour phase of this race.

2 **Greater Brazilian** or **Schuyl's Teal** *Amazonetta brasiliensis ipecutiri* VIEILLOT Argentina, south of Buenos Aires. The ranges of the races of *A. brasiliensis* are probably complicated by some migration.

3 **Australian Wood Duck** or **Maned Goose** *Chenonetta jubata* (LATHAM) Inland Australia.

4 **Mandarin Duck** *Aix galericulata* (L.) Eastern Asia from the Amur and Ussuri, south through Korea, eastern China, Japan to Taiwan. Introduced and now well established in England.

5 **North American Wood Duck** *Aix sponsa* (L.) Eastern half of the United States and southern Canada. Wintering in southern and south-eastern States. Also in the west from British Columbia to California (an entirely separate population).

6 **African Pygmy Goose** *Nettapus auritus* (BODDAERT) Africa from a line between Gambia and Kenya, south to the Cape along the coastal belt only, and Madagascar.

7 **Green Pygmy Goose** *Nettapus pulchellus* GOULD Southern Papua New Guinea, northern Australia.

8 **Indian Pygmy Goose** or **Cotton Teal** *Nettapus coromandelianus coromandelianus* (GMELIN) India, Sri Lanka, Burma, east to southern China, south to Malaysia and north-western Indonesia.

9 **Australian Pygmy Goose** *Nettapus coromandelianus albipennis* GOULD North-eastern Australia, nowhere abundant.

Dark Phase

♀
♂

Light Phase

♀
♂

1

1 and 2 intergrade

♀
♂

2

5

How to distinguish the females and eclipse plumage males of

♀

4

♂

from

5

Although apparently closely related no hybrid between 4 and 5 has been recorded, probably due to chromosome differences

4

♀
♂ with crest depressed

♂ with crest spread

3

♀
♂

8

♀
♂

9

♀
♂

Slightly larger than Indian race

6

♀
♂

7

♀
♂

P.S.

PLATE 19 PERCHING DUCKS AND GEESE

1 **Comb Duck** *Sarkidiornis melanotos melanotos* (PENNANT) Africa from Gambia and the Sudan, south to the Cape and Madagascar; India, Sri Lanka, Burma and south-eastern China.

2 **South American Comb Duck** *Saridiornis melanotos carunculatus* (LICHTENSTEIN) Eastern tropical South America from Venezuela, south to southern Brazil, Paraguay and northern Argentina.

3 **Western Hartlaub's Duck** *Pteronetta hartlaubi hartlaubi* (CASSIN) West and central Africa (Liberia eastwards; limits of range not known). Probably intergrades with *albifrons*.

4 **Eastern Hartlaub's Duck** *Pteronetta hartlaubi albifrons* (NEUMANN) African Lake Region and Congo westwards at least to Ituri River. Probably intergrades westward with *hartlaubi*.

5 **White-winged Wood Duck** *Cairina scutulata* (S. MÜLLER) Resident Assam, Bangladesh, Burma, Thailand and Sumatra, and possibly Malaysia and Java, where probably now extinct. Population in wild thought to number 400–450 (1995).

6 **Muscovy Duck** *Cairina moschata* (L.) Mexico, south through central America and South America to Peru on the west and to Uruguay in the east. The ancestor of the farmyard Muscovy Duck.

7 **Spur-winged Goose** *Plectropterus gambensis gambensis* (L.) Africa from Gambia to upper Nile, south to the Zambesi.

8 **Black Spur-winged Goose** *Plectropterus gambensis niger* P.L. SCLATER Africa, south of the Zambesi.

2

♀

♂

1

♀

♂

3

♀

♂

♂

4

5   ♂ and ♀
the same

Domestic Muscovy, which
may be glossy green, grey or
white, or a mixture

In both races there is
a carpal spur, larger
in the male. It is nor-
mally hidden

7

♀

♂

6

♀

♂

♀

♂

The species from which
the farmyard Muscovy
was originally domesticated

8

7 and 8 intergrade

P.S.

PLATE 20 SCOTERS

Tribe **Mergini**
(Scoters, Goldeneyes, Mergansers)

1 **†Labrador Duck** *Camptorhynchus labradorius* (GMELIN) Now extinct. Formerly bred in Labrador. Wintered south, probably to Chesapeake Bay, but chiefly off Long Island. Last one shot in 1875.

2 ***Common** or **Black Scoter** *Melanitta nigra nigra* (L.) Breeds in Iceland, Ireland, Scotland, northern Europe and Asia from Norway, east to the Taimyr Peninsula. Winters chiefly on coasts of western Europe (including Britain). Mediterranean, Black and Caspian Seas.

3 **American Black Scoter** *Melanitta nigra americana* (SWAINSON) Breeds in north-eastern Asia, Aleutian Islands, western Alaska, sporadically across northern North America to Newfoundland. Winters south to China and Japan, California, North Carolina, and on Great Lakes.

4 ***Surf Scoter** *Melanitta perspicillata* (L.) Breeds in northern North America, west of Hudson's Bay in Labrador and possibly in north-eastern Siberia. Winters from Alaska to California, on the Great Lakes, and from Nova Scotia to South Carolina. Occasional in Britain.

5 ***Velvet** or **European White-winged Scoter** *Melanitta fusca fusca* (L.) Breeds from Scandinavia and the Baltic, east to Yenisei. Winters on the coasts of western Europe (including Britain), the Mediterranean, Black and Caspian Seas.

6 **Asiatic White-winged Scoter** *Melanitta fusca stejnegeri* (RIDGWAY) Breeds in eastern Asia from the Altai to Anadyr, Kamchatka and the Commander Islands. Winters on Pacific coast south to China and Japan.

7 **Pacific White-winged Scoter** *Melanitta fusca dixoni* (BROOKS) Breeds in western Alaska. Winters on Pacific coast of North America, south to California. There is some considerable doubt whether this race can justifiably be separated from *deglandi*.

8 **American White-winged Scoter** *Melanitta fusca deglandi* (BONAPARTE) Breeds in north-western Canada from the Mackenzie to James Bay and south to North Dakota. Winters on the Great Lakes and Atlantic coast, south to North Carolina.

Nail of bill more curved in both sexes

♀
♂
♀
♂

3

2

Bills of drake Scoters

2

3

4

6

5

8

As above but shorter

7

Extinct

1

♀
♂

4

♀

♂

The females of all four races of Velvet Scoter are almost exactly alike

♂

♂

5

♀

♂

♂

7

8

6

P.S.

PLATE 21 HARLEQUINS, LONGTAIL AND GOLDENEYES

1 ***Atlantic Harlequin Duck** *Histrionicus histrionicus histrionicus* (L.) Iceland, Greenland, northern Labrador. Mainly resident, breeding on rivers and wintering on sea coasts; some south to Long Island in winter. Rare straggler to Britain.

2 **Pacific** or **Western Harlequin Duck** *Histrionicus histrionicus pacificus* W. S. BROOKS Breeds in eastern Siberia from the Lena and Lake Baikal to Anadyr, Kamchatka, Sakhalin and the Kurile Islands. In North America from southern Alaska, south in the mountains to central California and Colorado. Winters on coasts south to Japan and California. This race always doubtfully valid and now generally not recognised.

3 ***Long-tailed Duck** or **Old Squaw** *Clangula hyemalis* (L.) Breeds on Arctic coasts of Europe, Asia and North America. Winters south to Britain, France, Holland, Black Sea, Caspian Sea, Japan, California, the Great Lakes, North Carolina; southern Greenland.

4 ***Barrow's Goldeneye** *Bucephala islandica* (GMELIN) Breeds in Iceland, south-western Greenland, Labrador and in the mountains of north-western North America from south-central Alaska to south-western Colorado. The birds of Iceland and Greenland are resident, repairing to the coast in winter. Those in America winter south to Long Island on the Atlantic coast and San Francisco on the Pacific. Females with largely yellow bills occur often in the Rocky Mountain population but apparently not in the other parts of the breeding range.

5 ***European Goldeneye** *Bucephala clangula clangula* (L.) Breeds from northern Scandinavia east across Europe and Asia, north to the limit of trees, south to Germany, Balkans, central Russia and Siberia to Kamchatka and Sakhalin. Winters from British Isles, Mediterranean, northern India, to southern China and Japan. Now breeds in Scotland.

6 **American Goldeneye** *Bucephala clangula americana* (BONAPARTE) Breeds in North America in heavy timber from Alaska and British Columbia to Newfoundland. Winters on Pacific coast south to California and on Atlantic to South Carolina. Also on open lakes and rivers in central United States.

7 ***Bufflehead** *Bucephala albeola* (L.) Breeds from central Alaska to Hudson's Bay, south to British Columbia, Alberta and Manitoba. Winters mainly in the United States; also Aleutian and Commander Islands. Rare vagrant to Britain.

Darker chestnut streak

♂

2

1

Races doubtfully
valid

♀

♀

♂

♂

1

Paler
streak

White goes
farther back

Heavier bill

♂

2

Slightly larger bird

The Longtail has two strikingly
different plumages – summer and
winter (and an eclipse in the
drake in autumn)

♀

3

♂

Summer

♀ showing
wholly yellow bill

Winter

♀

♂

♂

♀

4

♀

♂

♂

♀

6

Larger

♂

5

Smaller

♀

♂

7

P.S.

PLATE 22 MERGANSERS OR SAWBILLS

1 ***Smew** *Mergus albellus* L. Breeds in Europe and Asia from Scandinavia to Siberia and south to the Volga, Turkestan and the Amur. Winters on coasts and lakes from Britain (regular on reservoirs near London), the Mediterranean, Iran, northern India to China and Japan.

2 ***Hooded Merganser** *Mergus cucullatus* L. North America, breeding from south central Canada to southern U.S. and wintering chiefly in the Pacific States, Great Lakes, the Gulf States and Atlantic States south of New York. Rare vagrant to Britain.

3 **Brazilian Merganser** *Mergus octosetaceus* VIEILLOT Southern Brazil, eastern Paraguay and north-eastern Argentina. Now very rare.

4 **†Auckland Islands Merganser** *Mergus australis* HOMBRON & JACQUINOT Found on Auckland Islands (250 miles south of New Zealand) from 1840 to 1902, but not since. Sub-fossil bones also found on east coast of South Island, New Zealand.

5 ***Red-breasted Merganser** *Mergus serrator serrator* L. Breeds in suitable places throughout northern Europe, Asia, and North America (including British Isles), south in winter to the Mediterranean, Persian Gulf, China, Taiwan, Gulf of Mexico and Florida.

6 **Greenland Merganser** *Mergus serrator schioleri* SALOMONSEN Resident in Greenland. This race no longer generally recognised.

7 **Chinese** or **Scaly-sided Merganser** *Mergus squamatus* GOULD Breeds south-eastern Russia, north-western China (Manchuria) and North Korea. Winters in China from western Szechuan to central Fukien and south to western Yunnan.

8 ***Goosander** *Mergus merganser merganser* L. Breeds in Europe and Asia from Iceland, British Isles, Switzerland, the Balkans, to Kamchatka, the Kurile and Commander Islands. South in winter to Mediterranean and China.

9 **Asiatic Goosander** *Mergus merganser orientalis* GOULD Afghanistan, Turkestan, Altai, Tibet. Winters northern India, northern Burma and China (Szechuan) and farther east, where it occurs with the typical race.

10 **American Merganser** *Mergus merganser americanus* CASSIN North America, breeding south of a line from south-eastern Alaska to James Bay; and wintering south to the Gulf of Mexico.

2 ♀ ♂

1 ♀ ♂

6 ♀
Thicker bill

♂

5 ♀ ♂

5

8

Greenland race no
longer recognised

10 ♀ ♂

♂

♀

Nail hooked

♂

9
Smaller

8

7 ♀
♂

3

♂

♀ had single
white wing bar

♂ and ♀ similar

4
Extinct

P.S.

PLATE 23 STIFFTAILS

Tribe **Oxyurini**

1 **Masked Duck** Oxyura dominica (L.) Greater Antilles (Cuba, Haiti, Jamaica, Puerto Rico) and South America to central Chile and north-eastern Argentina.

2 **White-headed Duck** Oxyura leucocephala (SCOPOLI) Breeds southern Spain and Tunisia (where resident) and Turkey east through Kazahkstan to north-east China. Latter population winters from Turkey to Pakistan.

3 **North American Ruddy Duck** Oxyura jamaicensis jamaicensis (GMELIN) Breeds in north-west central North America and winters south to California, Mexico, Florida and the Carolinas; also resident in West Indies. Birds escaped from captivity have established a thriving population in Britain.

4 **Colombian Ruddy Duck** Oxyura jamaicensis andina LEHMANN Andean lakes of central and eastern Colombia. This race forms the link between O.j. jamaicensis and O.j. ferruginea and may intergrade in both directions.

5 **Peruvian Ruddy Duck** Oxyura jamaicensis ferruginea (EYTON) Breeds from southern Colombia down full length of Andes through Peru, eastern Bolivia, Chile and Argentina to Tierra del Fuego.

6 **Argentine Ruddy Duck** Oxyura vittata (R. A. PHILIPPI) Southern South America from northern Chile and southern Brazil to Tierra del Fuego. This species and O.j. ferruginea have been found breeding on the Lago Peñuelas, near Valparaíso, which indicates that they must be regarded as specifically distinct.

7 **Australian Blue-billed Duck** Oxyura australis (GOULD) In dense swamps in southern Australia.

8 **Maccoa Duck** Oxyura maccoa (EYTON) Eastern Africa from southern Ethiopia to the Cape.

9 **Musk Duck** Biziura lobata (SHAW) Southern Australia and Tasmania; in deep, permanent swamps.

10 **African White-backed Duck** Thalassornis leuconotus leuconotus EYTON Africa from eastern Cameroon and southern Ethiopia, south to the Cape.

11 **Madagascar White-backed Duck** Thalassornis leuconotus insularis RICHMOND Madagascar.

12 **Black-headed Duck** Heteronetta atricapilla (MERREM) Central Chile, east to Paraguay and southern Brazil, south in Argentina at least to the latitude of Buenos Aires.

Recent behavioural and anatomical work suggests that the genus Thalassornis may be more closely related to the tribe Dendrocygnini than to the Oxyurini.

Two normal swimming positions

♂ displaying

Tail spread

3

♀

♂

2

Winter ♂

♀

1

♀

♂

Summer ♂

Broad bill

♀

♂

4

5

These three races intergrade, the white cheeks (not always present in **4**) are progressively lost

♀

♂

♀

♂

6

8

7

Narrow bill

♀

♂

10

♂ and ♀ the same

11

Normal swimming position

Smaller and brighter ♂ and ♀ the same

♀

12

♂

9

Parasitic, laying in other bird's nests

P.S.

INDEX OF SCIENTIFIC NAMES

Figures opposite names refer to plate numbers. Names of genera are shown in **bold**, of species and subspecies in roman type. Where a species includes several subspecies the subspecific name only is cited with that of the genus: e.g., *Dendrocygna arcuata arcuata* is listed as 'arcuata, Dendrocygna' while *Dendrocygna arcuata australis* appears as 'australis, Dendrocygna'. The names of genera and species shown in parenthesis are synonyms no longer in use. Only names which have been widely used, but are now discarded, are included in the synonymy.

INDEX OF ENGLISH NAMES

The application of English names to birds is not governed by formal procedure such as governs the scientific terminology. This index is correspondingly unsystematic. It aims at enabling the reader to find the illustrations of every species, and so it includes a number of names in local or general use even though alternative names have been employed in the text. Such additional names are shown in italic type, followed immediately by the preferred name, in roman type.

Although it seemed desirable to provide in the text a distinctive English name for every subspecies, these lengthy names are rarely used, the specific name being the obvious choice. Accordingly in this index only the specific vernacular names are given except in those cases where one subspecies has acquired a distinctive English name of its own. For example, twelve races of Canada Goose are illustrated on plate 5: in this index all are covered by the entry 'Canada Goose', but 'Cackling Goose' is also included, because this bird is not generally known as the 'Cackling Canada Goose'.

A few names not originally English have also been included, e.g., 'Ne-ne' for the Hawaiian Goose, familiarity being the criterion.

THE WILDFOWL
AND WETLANDS TRUST

Sir Peter Scott founded The Wildfowl & Wetlands Trust (WWT) on the banks of the River Severn at Slimbridge in Gloucestershire in 1946. His aim was 'to establish a centre for the scientific study, public display and conservation of the wildfowl of the world'.

WWT is the only wildlife conservation charity in the UK dedicated to wetlands and their wildlife. It carries out its work through programmes of conservation, education, research and recreation. With eight visitor centres around the UK, WWT aims to bring people of all ages and abilities into contact with wetlands and their wildlife.

Two derelict cottages near the small Gloucestershire village of Slimbridge on the Severn Estuary formed WWT's first 'headquarters' with four wartime defence pill boxes acting as hides from which to observe wild birds. From these early beginnings, the organisation has grown into one which employs around 180 staff and manages over 4,000 acres of wetland habitat (including six Sites of Special Scientific Interest and five Ramsar sites).

Wetlands – habitats where land and water meet, such as ponds, lakes, rivers, peatlands, estuaries and the seashore – are vital to the survival of many plants and animals including dragonflies, fish, frogs and otters and the birds which have been at the heart of WWT's work: swans, geese and ducks. They are also vital to our own survival, providing water and many foods, as well as services such as flood and erosion protection and places for recreation.

Yet wetlands are threatened by pollution, drainage, agriculture and development. WWT is committed to securing a safer future for wetlands so that they can continue to support the survival of both wildlife and man.

WWT Centres

WWT Centres are all different, but all are designed to meet the needs of both visitors and wildlife. The sites were chosen for their value to wetland wildlife and developed to share this wildlife with people. Visit a WWT Centre at different times of the year and you will be guaranteed a different visit every time. The landscape constantly changes, the colourful yellow, red and purple hues of wetland flowers in mid-summer giving way to hoarfrost magnificently decorating the trees in winter.

There are changes among the birds too, with the arrival and departure of thousands of migratory ducks, geese and swans throughout the year. In spring, birds take part in courtship rituals, showing off their magnificent plumage. From late spring until mid-summer, hatching is in full swing at most of the Centres with delightful fluffy ducklings, goslings and cygnets all over the grounds. Additionally, all but two of the Centres have tame wildfowl from around the world, many of which are so friendly, they will even feed from your hand. These include rare species, which WWT is helping to save from extinction.

WWT Centres provide excellent facilities for all visitors. These include birdwatching from well-designed hides and observatories, shops and restaurants, events programmes of walks, talks and school holiday activities, exhibits and interpretation of wildfowl and wetland issues and educational programmes for schools and universities. WWT's education staff currently works with around 75,000 schoolchildren a year and develops a wide range of materials and activities related to the National Curriculum.

At **WWT Slimbridge**, large flocks of wild birds, including thousands of White-fronted Geese, several hundred Bewick's Swans and many different species of duck, return every winter to the protection and security of the reserve. Over 800 acres of fields and salt marsh are managed specifically for the wildfowl. An extensive system of hides allows visitors to watch the birds without disturbing them. Visitors can also walk among tame wildfowl – one of the most colourful and diverse collections in the world. The Centre boasts a Tropical House and is the only place in Europe where all six types of flamingo can be seen.

WWT Martin Mere is the most important wintering site for Pink-footed Geese in the UK – over 25,000 return to the Centre every year from their Icelandic breeding grounds, joining hundreds of Bewick's and Whooper Swans and thousands of ducks. In 1985, Martin Mere was designated a Wetland of International Importance under the Ramsar convention, an international agreement to protect wetlands and the wildlife they support. The collection at Martin Mere also features flocks of Chilean and Greater Flamingos.

WWT Washington in Tyne and Wear, is set in a shallow valley sloping down to the River Wear. Visitors can get close to hundreds of birds, including the rare Hawaiian Goose or Nene. Wild birds, which often use the lakes and pools as 'stopovers' during their annual migrations, can be observed from hides and the wild bird feeding station is a great spot to catch a glimpse of Great Spotted Woodpecker, Smew, Goldeneye and

Wigeon. The Centre also has a wild Heronry, where visitors can observe these birds at extremely close quarters through a special closed circuit television system.

A beautiful wooded hillside and large castle form a magnificent backdrop to **WWT Arundel** in West Sussex. Landscaped lakes and meadows lie in a picturesque setting between the River Arun and Swanbourne Lake. Wildfowl, especially diving ducks, thrive in the fresh, clear spring waters. On the refuge, observation hides overlook wader scrapes and a splendid reed bed – designated a SSSI because of its importance to warblers – sheltering many birds, including Water Rail, Teal, Snipe, Greenshank, Redshank and Green Sandpiper.

Set in a traditional industrial area of South Wales, **WWT Llanelli** is an example of conservation and industry working together. Located on the Burry Inlet, a SSSI, the reserve attracts an incredible diversity of wading birds. Spotted Redshank, Curlew, Oystercatcher, Greenshank and Lapwing can all be seen, along with Little Egret, Kingfisher, Pintail, Shoveler, Wigeon, Teal, Gadwall and even the occasional Osprey. The Centre is also home to many tame wildfowl and a flock of colourful Caribbean Flamingos.

On the shores of Strangford Lough in County Down, **WWT Castle Espie** welcomes up to 15,000 Light-bellied Brent Geese every winter. The Centre is also home to a delightful collection of ducks, geese and swans and features an art gallery and four activity areas with displays, games and simple experiments.

Imagine the sound of a 14,000-strong dawn chorus building to a crescendo as Barnacle Geese fly from their evening roost. Visitors can hear and see such a spectacle at **WWT Caerlaverock** on the shores of the Solway Firth in Dumfriesshire. This vital wetland area is the winter home to the entire Svalbard population of Barnacle Geese. After the war, only 300 Barnacle Geese wintered on the Solway, but following the opening of the Centre in 1971, numbers have increased to an astonishing 14,000. The refuge also attracts thousands of Pink-footed Geese, Wigeon, Pintail, Teal, Bewick's and Whooper Swans, and large numbers of waders, and nesting Barn Owls can be observed on a CCTV system.

WWT Welney, on the Ouse Washes in Norfolk, is the most important site in Europe for wintering Bewick's and Whooper Swans. Pair bonding rituals, preening, feeding and even the occasional squabble take place just a few feet from visitors sitting in comfort in a centrally-heated observatory. During winter, the Centre also welcomes thousands of Pochard, Wigeon, Pintail, Teal, Gadwall and Shoveler, while in summer, residents include

Garganey, Teal, Black-tailed Godwits, and occasional Black Terns.

Recent developments at Centres include a Wetland Discovery Centre at Washington, Activity Centres at Arundel and Pond Zones at Martin Mere and Slimbridge. These combine technology (CD ROMS and computer games) with activities such as pond dipping, handling of artefacts, and arts and crafts sessions.

WWT is currently working on two exciting projects for the millennium – a redevelopment at Slimbridge, which will provide a new restaurant, shop, entrance area, Ecological Discovery Centre, Sustainable Garden, Observation Tower and Conservation Enquiry office, and a brand new Centre – The Wetland Centre – in the heart of London.

Research & Conservation

For conservation programmes to be effective, information is continually needed about migration patterns, fluctuations in wildfowl populations and changes in the wetland habitat, as well as basic animal behaviour and ecology. The experience gained over the last 50 years and the quality of the data collected by the research team at Slimbridge is such that help and practical advice is sought by and given to organisations, agencies and governments all over the world. The team also coordinates the efforts of over 2,000 ornithologists in Britain and Ireland, collecting information about waterbirds and wetlands; develops techniques for the creation and restoration of wetland habitats; and plans for the conservation of threatened species. Expert ecological consultancy services are provided through WWT's Wetlands Advisory Service (WAS).

Conservation work at Centres includes habitat creation and management. Summers are spent managing various types of wetland habitat so that returning migratory wildfowl find food and shelter during the winter. WWT Centres are important for wildlife other than wildfowl. WWT Caerlaverock is the most northern location for a population of the globally threatened Natterjack Toad; Common Frogs have been re-established on the Ouse Washes at WWT Welney; good numbers of the threatened Water Vole can be seen at WWT Slimbridge and all Centres have a diverse population of wild birds. Several nationally rare plants are found on WWT reserves.

Education & Public Awareness

Apart from programmes for schools, WWT seeks to provide opportunities for people of all ages and interests to discover more about nature through events and exhibits, and to learn how they can help support WWT's causes, for example by creating a wildlife pond at home or incorporating water saving measures into daily lifestyles.

WWT's 'Wetland Link International' (WLI) programme, with contacts in more than 100 countries, seeks to increase effective contact between the growing number of wetland education/conservation centres around the world. Topics covered include educational programmes, training courses and designs for new centres. WLI produces a biannual newsletter for its participants and helps them to locate relevant expertise and exchange ideas.

WWT is leading efforts to develop a global programme of education and public awareness about wetlands, in partnership with the Ramsar Convention and Wetlands International. In the UK, WWT is taking a lead in developing education and public awareness programmes in support of biodiversity.

How you can help

WWT is a registered charity which needs your help to continue conserving wildfowl and wetlands. Contact your local Centre for further details on how you can help, or information about opening hours and admission prices.

WWT Slimbridge, The Wildfowl & Wetlands Trust, Slimbridge, Gloucester, GL2 7BT. Telephone: 01453 890333

WWT Arundel, The Wildfowl & Wetlands Trust, Mill Road, Arundel, Sussex, BN18 9PB. Telephone: 01903 883355

WWT Caerlaverock, The Wildfowl & Wetlands Trust, Eastpark Farm, Caerlaverock, Dumfriesshire, DG1 4RS. Telephone: 01387 77200

WWT Castle Espie, The Wildfowl & Wetlands Trust, 78 Ballydrain Road, Comber, Newtownards, Co. Down, BT23 6EA. Telephone: 01247 874146

WWT Llanelli, The Wildfowl & Wetlands Trust, Penclacwydd, Llanelli, Dyfed, SA14 9SH. Telephone: 01554 741087

WWT Martin Mere, The Wildfowl & Wetlands Trust, Burscough, Ormskirk, Lancashire, L40 OTA. Telephone: 01704 895181

WWT Washington, The Wildfowl & Wetlands Trust, District 15, Washington, Tyne & Wear, NE38 8LE. Telephone: 0191 416 5454

WWT Welney, The Wildfowl & Wetlands Trust, Hundred Foot Bank, Welney, Nr. Wisbech, Cambridgeshire, PE14 9TN. Telephone: 01353 860711

WWT The Wetland Centre, Barn Elms Lodge, Queen Elizabeth Walk, Barnes, London, SW1 0DB. Telephone: 0181 876 8995